Endorsements from Tammy's Clients

(Names are limited to first or fictitious names in order to remain confidential.)

I was so burdened from painful things people had said to me or done to me over the years that I was barely functioning. I was so full of pain I no longer knew who I was. Tammy would pray and ask what God was saying to me. Amazing to me, each time He was actually giving me an answer! Every answer sounded so simple that I was surprised I hadn't thought of it myself! But it truly was the Holy Spirit answering and releasing me from the pain I carried from each issue! God used Tammy Melton not only to help me forgive but to understand that I am a significant part of God's plan! And - I am FORGIVEN!! - **Judy**

Tammy has taught me to let go of hurts, pains, and wounds that held me back and kept me in the enemy's strongholds. Through this process I have learned to reach for the Lord in times of distress and ask Him what He wants for me to see or hear from the situation. I know this book will start you on the path to freedom in Christ. By following Tammy's teaching, I walked through a revival and learned to listen to the Holy Spirit and not the enemy! - **Penny**

Tammy Melton has played a huge part in adding value to the relationships in my life! She has helped me in my relationship with God, to learn to trust Him in a deeper level I had not experienced before and to worry less. She has helped in my relationship with my husband, to be a voice of peace in times of extreme stress, and to help us grow in our love, communication and understanding for each other. She has also helped in my relationship with myself, helping me to recognize that self-care is just as important as caring for others. I am incredibly thankful for the gift God has given her and that she has used that gift to impact my life in such a great way! - **Kim**

Through Tammy's spiritual and biblical guidance, I was able to see the harm my addictions were causing in my walk with Christ and in my marriage. Her leadership and direction has helped our marriage and taught us to how to repair damage done, and we are seeing the sweetness and love come back to our marriage. It's amazing how God has used her to help us and others, and we are thankful for her wisdom and love she has shown to us. - **Lowell**

As a Pastor, having therapy sessions with Tammy has been essential in giving me the time and space to work on the things that matter most to me as a wife, mother, and leader in the church. Not only does she give me perspective about my relationships with others, but she also guides me to see what God wants in each relationship. This has been especially helpful in times of spiritual warfare. The depth of my prayer life has increased exponentially because of her guidance. I'm eternally grateful and can't say enough about how powerful my time with her has been. - **Shannon**

Tammy Melton's teaching has been life changing—you can feel the presence of the Holy Spirit in her practical and Biblically-based teachings and counseling. Tammy's counseling has strengthened my marriage and how we look at our situation. It has helped us to realize that God is in control, and we have to relinquish control to Him. - **Dwain**

Other Endorsements

So many Christians today struggle through life, not knowing the transforming power of the Holy Spirit. Jesus promised us abundant life, but so few of us venture away from the shore to explore His deeper waters. That's why I'm so grateful for Tammy Melton and her counseling and teaching ministry. She is calling the church to take the risks to go deeper with God. Her book *Refining Relationships* will help any Christian venture into maturity. And she makes it clear that the process of spiritual growth is not an isolated journey—we need other people in our lives to help us grow. I pray you will take all the risks necessary to follow Tammy's advice. The abundant life will be yours.

J. Lee Grady
Director, The Mordecai Project
LaGrange, Georgia
www.themordecaiproject.org

Refining Relationships by Tammy Melton, LPC is a harmonious blend of insightful psychology and rich Biblical truths. The message is crucial, her research is fascinating and the take-aways are highly impactful. Relationships take work and intentionality. This work on relationships provides practical tools and attainable goals that would be of benefit to every reader. To make an effective impact for the Kingdom of God, we need to be able to love well and make our relationships a priority. What an important work for such a time as this!

Pastor Rhonda McGinnis, Executive Pastor
Trinity Church, Sharpsburg, GA
www.tri-church.com

Tammy Melton is my "go to" resource when I refer individuals for further assistance after an initial crisis intervention event. My respect for her comes not only from the credentials she holds, but the way she holds them as a "work-in-progress," simply passing along to others the challenging lessons she too has had to learn. In *Refining Relationships*, Tammy identifies the obstacles of misunderstanding and disappointment that create barriers to better relationships. This book provides the reader with the tools to more intimate relationships, filled with hope and purpose by pointing us to the perfect example we find in Christ. I look forward to adding this book to my tool kit for application within my own relationships and in my work with others.

Kenneth Koon, D.Min, President
Armed Forces Mission
AFMFamily.com

This book is so needed in today's world! Every individual, pastor, business owner, friend, and parent needs the tools given by Tammy in *Refining Relationships*. These relationship principles will bring healing if you're willing to walk them out. Trust me, I'm one of those set free!

Rev. Doreen Ferguson, Co-Pastor
The River Foursquare Church, Naugatuck, CT
www.theriveralive.org

Refining Relationships is an insightful work that focuses on improving self and on building healthy, successful relationships with God and with others. Tammy Melton is a gifted author who appropriately and humbly shares some of her own personal experiences of growth and understanding. As a skillful teacher and counselor, she stimulates her readers to desire their own personal growth and maturity. She provides practical illustrations and good assessment tools that guide the reader to measurable and attainable goals. Her profound understanding of scripture allows her to weave her work with words of Biblical wisdom, helping and encouraging us to examine our hearts and our motives in our personal relationships.

Rev. Karen L DeJong, Pastoral Counselor, Co/Founder
Grace Connection Ministry, Naples, FL
www.graceconnection.org

I began reading, and it quickly had a read on me. I could not put it down!

Richard Sharp, Operation Mobilization Missionary
Founder of One Wish, Tyrone, GA,
www.onewish4u.org

Melton stretches our thinking about relationships as she tackles some of the key relational challenges. She gives us the tools needed to cultivate healthy relationships with God, self, and others. As you read this book - two things will happen: 1) You will feel your heart healing from previous unhealthy relationships and 2) You will no longer view your relationship through the lens of being the victim, but rather from a place of victory!

JC Worley, Lead Pastor
GO Church, Atlanta, GA
www.mygochurch.com

Refining Relationships By Tammy Melton, LPC, is a must have for any home library! This book is an amazing handbook and guidance for any relationship. We all are individually created by God, and every one of us could use help in relating to others effectively. Tammy presents Godly solutions to relationship issues based on the Word of God and the example of Jesus Christ, along with her training as a Licensed Professional Counselor. Upon your completion of reading this book, you will already experience more peace concerning any relationship in your life!

Van and Regina Smith, Founders and Pastors
The Solid Rock of Atlanta
www.TheSolidRockofAtlanta.org

Why should you read this book? Let me tell you why: Tammy puts a great deal of herself in this text, encapsulating her decades of caring experience, knowledge, and wisdom. Tammy offers the reader principles discussed only by those possessing a life-calling from the Holy Spirit in the ministry of guiding the brokenhearted to the healing of God's amazing grace.

Michael R Cooley, Christian Executive Consultant
MRC Consulting Group LLC, Atlanta
www.michaelrcooley.com

Relationships are the basis on which the kingdom of God expands throughout the earth, and it is imperative that followers of Jesus make right relationships a priority. Tammy Melton has written a masterful manual that will help the reader have a proper perspective on the importance of living life intentionally and to allow all of their relationships to be refined.

Pastor Tom Herbert, Lead Pastor
Freedom Community Church, Shrewsbury, PA
www.calledtofreedom.org

A well-written book that will feed your mind, soul and spirit, leave you feeling empowered and make you more equipped at refining any relationship in your life. A licensed professional counselor and an ordained minister, Tammy Melton proficiently demonstrates how to improve relationships God's way by teaching practical techniques from a Biblical platform. A profoundly useful tool for anyone seeking lasting peace, hope and joy in relationships. Job well done!

Shaw Wendi Fortuchang, MD, FAPA
Co-Owner and Co-Founder of The Fort Christian Psychiatric Center,
Fayetteville, GA
www.thefortchristian.com

Relationships take hard work, dedication, and with the right framework, we can experience healing in our relationship with God, self, and others. In *Refining Relationships*, Tammy weaves together a beautiful picture of what really works in keeping our relationships strong and healthy while identifying where we can improve. This is a must read book!

Jason Sisam, Author, Pastor, and Writing Coach
Minneapolis, MN
www.jbsisam.com

REFINING
RELATIONSHIPS

To Scott & Lynn -
Thank you for your
hospitality. I pray this
book will be a blessing to you.

In Christ,

Jimmy

Eph. 3:20-21

REFINING RELATIONSHIPS

WITH GOD, SELF, AND OTHERS

TAMMY MELTON, LPC

LEGACY
FREEDOM
PUBLICATIONS

Cover and book design: Jason Sisam with Living Lights Media
livinglightsmedia.com | jbsisam.com

The publisher is not responsible for websites (or their content) that are not owned by the publisher.

ISBN: 978-0-578-52291-3 (Print Edition)

Printed in the United States of America

2019

11 10 9 8 7 6 5 4 3 2

I would like to dedicate this book in memory of my dear father-in-law, Rev. Ralph Melton. Dad never met a stranger. He could engage people in conversation better than anyone I know. While he was never at a loss for words, he made sure he asked about the other person and how they were doing instead of just talking about himself. During his forty-plus years as a pastor, he not only talked freely with both strangers and friends, but he also took time to mentor many people with his God-given wisdom. During times when trials of ministry discouraged me, Dad encouraged God's call on my life to be a woman in ministry and helped motivate me to never quit. I will forever be grateful to God for allowing me to be Ralph Melton's daughter-in-love!

CONTENTS

FOREWORD

> *How blessed is the man who finds wisdom,*
> *And the man who gains understanding.*
>
> — *Proverbs 3:13 (NASB)*

"Savvy" is the intersection of wisdom and knowledge. When Paul went to Athens, he operated with **savvy** as he used **knowledge** of the culture of the city and **wisdom** in making that knowledge a bridge for the message of the Good News of Jesus Christ. Tammy Melton has written a book full of savvy in dealing with relationships.

Refining Relationships is practically applicable in bringing the Biblical Christian Worldview to relationships. Tammy discusses the practical truths of relationships and how God's truth is the root of all healthy relationships. Thirty-plus years of ministry and counseling have helped her to refine her savvy of the realm of relationships, what is detrimental to relationships and what brings them healing and life. If you read this book and implement the principles she shares, you will be refined. And the truth is, all of us need refinement.

Tammy has a passion for people to live their lives in harmony with each other and in symphony with God. She wants the best for you, so she has written this book to **Make Life Better**.

In *Refining Relationships*, you will find interactive surveys to assess your relationships, diagrams to visualize relational interactions and prayers to actualize the wisdom and knowledge you gain.

As a lead pastor, I plan to take my Gathering through this book in a message series. I think every person will benefit from the Biblically-based truths which Tammy presents in a useful way. This is a book that will change lives by **Refining Relationships**.

Dr. Bob Swanger

President

Harvest Network International

www.harvestnetworkintl.org

INTRODUCTION

T HE IDEA FOR this book came when I was asked to present a workshop at the 2018 National Assembly for Harvest Network, International. The theme for the conference was "Uplift." As I pondered what topic I could teach to go along with the theme, I thought about how relationships have extreme power in our lives to either build one another up or weigh each other down. Dysfunctional relationships can even foster feelings that life itself has been drained from our beings. One of my passions is to promote healthy relationships that can: lift one another up; improve one another socially, intellectually, and morally; and encourage healthy emotions and spiritual growth. These ideas influenced my decision to teach a workshop on relationships.

I gathered so much information for the workshop that I soon realized I needed to write a book. I titled the workshop "Reinforcing Relationships" and was going to title the book the same. However, after some consideration, I decided to change the title; many people are reinforcing their relationships already, but they are reinforcing dysfunction rather than healthy function. I see it frequently in counseling sessions—especially sessions for marriage counseling. Each partner comes in telling me what he/she thinks is going on from his/her perspective, but the two perspectives do not align. Rather than providing constructive feedback to one another in order to combat misunderstandings, they seem to speak different languages. Sadly, their relationship gets stuck in a stalemate.

I chose *Refining Relationships* as the title in order to bring more clarification. All of our relationships can be refined, even the healthy ones. Rather than simply reinforcing relationships, the term "refine" brings an element of purity. I love the Cambridge Dictionary's definition: *"refine: v. to make a substance pure by removing unwanted material: To refine something also means to improve it by making small changes."*[1] This definition implies the idea of removing impurities, but it also implies making small changes to improve quality in something—namely, for the sake of this book, relationships.

When gold is purified, it is melted with extreme heat so that all the impurities rise to the top and are skimmed off. When our family toured a gold mine in the province of Quebec, Canada, I remember the tour guide saying that the last impurity to rise to the surface when refining gold is silver. Maybe you have a relationship you consider to be great like silver, but God is allowing you to go through a refining process so it will be even more pure like gold.

This book will examine what it means to refine relationships with God, self, and others. I will also describe interventions I use in counseling individuals, couples, and families as a professional Christian counselor.

By presenting this information, I am not suggesting that I have mastered these skills in my own life—I am also a work-in-progress. Basically, I am teaching you what God is teaching me in my own relationships and through my clients in therapy sessions. What a privilege it is to see God at work in reconciliation! My prayer is that this book will spark hope in you and give you tools to help you build healthy connections with God, self, and others.

NOTE:

- Stories of clients are only included if permission was given. Names are left out to ensure privacy. Some stories are fictitious and not intended to be about anyone in particular.
- Third person pronouns depicting gender can apply to all. She/her and he/him are used interchangeably.
- This book is not intended to take the place of a professional therapist's counsel or a medical doctor's advice in response to your specific situation. It is also not intended to provide the means of diagnosis for any mental or physical illness.

1

THE POWER OF PERSPECTIVE IN RELATIONSHIPS

perspective[1] [per-**spek**-tiv]
(noun)

The state of one's ideas, the facts known to one, etc.,
in having a meaningful interrelationship.

THE WORLD WOULD be a better place if we could resolve misunderstandings between people! What causes misunderstandings? The main answer is simple: perspective differences. Our perspectives shape the way we perceive situations. For example, someone raised in the southern United States is taught to treat older people with respect. Southerners say, "Yes, ma'am" or "No, sir" as a sign of honor. However, someone raised in the northern United States may be offended if someone calls them "ma'am" or "sir" because they do not want to be thought of as old. Unfortunately, one person's actions meant to promote respect can be misunderstood as offensive.

Before you continue reading, I encourage you to look at Figure 1-1 and contemplate how each of these areas has influenced your interactions with other people.

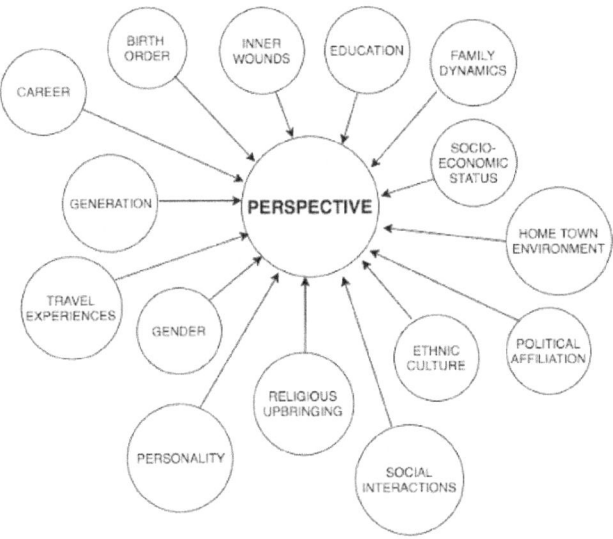

Figure 1-1

No one else shares your personal experiences; thus, no one else can bring what you bring to a relationship. Likewise, God intentionally places specific people in your life because of what they bring to you. When we consider perspective differences according to their benefit to us, we will celebrate each person's unique qualities instead of being critical of those who do not share our same perspective.

If we stay stuck in our own perspective, we will likely build walls between us and the people who do not share our same viewpoint. Since everyone has a different point of view, we cannot expect others to see things exactly as we see them. I have personally come to realize the importance of seeking God to show me my own perspective, the person's perspective with whom I have conflict, and, more importantly, God's perspective. The good news is that "in his own body on the cross, [Jesus] broke down the wall of hostility that separated us."[2] When we allow God to tear down walls between us, we will see how He can then build incredible connections with others. If we place Jesus as the cornerstone in each of our relationships *and* let Him build each relationship, we will then be "built together for a dwelling place of God in the Spirit."[3]

In the Christian faith there are many paradoxes, statements that seem to contradict. For instance, if you want to be great in God's Kingdom, you have to be a servant,[4] and he who loses his life for God will find it.[5] Likewise, we first have to tear down walls in order to build healthy relationships.[6] Although healthy boundaries between people are sometimes necessary, walls we build to defend our own perspectives need to come down. Otherwise, these walls will keep us from seeing the other person's point of view, thus perpetuating the cycle of misunderstanding and disappointment.

It may help to remember that relationships develop over time. Living life together is a journey with many steps to enjoy along the way. When we allow God to clarify perspectives, we will not only enjoy each step of our relationships, but we will also realize the importance of setting goals for them. As we do, we will believe in hope that the goals can be accomplished, add discipline to see the progress, and celebrate accomplishments along the way.

The Importance of Setting Goals in Relationships

Figure 1-2

Counselors are trained to help clients set **goals** that are measurable and attainable. To get a better understanding of how this works, let's look at a goal that is easily measured. Think about the process of losing weight. While many people contemplate the need to lose weight, most will fail without a concrete goal and a plan of action. A person who plans specifically to start by losing five pounds has a greater chance of reaching his goal than someone who simply wants to lose weight. Once a goal is set, he needs to have **hope** that he can and *will* reach that goal. However, he must apply **discipline** to accompany that hope. Achieving a goal is hard work. He has to adjust many things, including his diet, exercise routine, time management, and financial budget. Rather than merely saying he needs to lose weight, he will soon reach his first goal. This calls for a **celebration**! A good celebration will bring satisfaction of completion and inspire a grateful mindset. It will also spur hope to set the next goal of five more pounds with determination in his journey to reach his ideal weight.

Goals

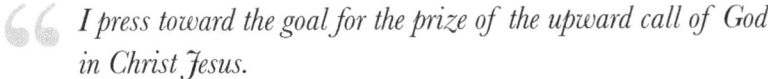

> *I press toward the goal for the prize of the upward call of God in Christ Jesus.*
>
> — PHILIPPIANS 3:14

Setting goals helps to facilitate progress in both dysfunctional and healthy relationships. Remember, even great relationships can be refined. Goals need to be measurable in order to identify completion. Measuring weight is easy, since the scale provides a concrete number. With a relationship, goal-setting is a little more complicated. Let's say your long-range goal is to have a better relationship with a loved one. The best-case scenario would be for both of you to work together to set goals for the relationship. Obviously, it takes two people in a relationship to make a functional, healthy connection, and you cannot make goals for the other person. Many times the other person will not be as eager to make changes. He may even blame you for all the problems between the two of you. You can still make goals for your side of the relationship regarding how you handle interactions with the other person and how you manage your own emotions. Amazingly, I have seen situations where one person's transformation actually inspired change within the other. Sadly, I have also witnessed cases where the broken relationship did not mend, and the client had to cut ties with the other person rather than allowing continued inner turmoil. If you find yourself in a similar position, the process of applying personal goals, hope, and discipline will cause you to have a healthy perspective so that you can separate from the other person and still have peace and healing.

One common goal I like to help clients set is to not be so controlled by negative emotions. One's emotions will greatly influence the conflicts within a relationship. I often hear clients blame their spouse, child, supervisor, etc. for their dysfunctional situation.

"So, are you saying he/she 'pushes your button' to get you upset?"

"Yes, that is exactly what I am saying!"

"What if you allowed God to heal you to the point where you don't have that button any more?"

"That would be great!"

I love it when a client comes in and exclaims, "My spouse (child, supervisor, etc.) did the same action, and it didn't bother me like it used to!" Now, *that* is a measurable goal accomplished!

Those "buttons" are usually caused by negative or traumatic experiences with people throughout our lifetime. Identifying negative emotions that are triggered when your buttons are pushed will help you initiate the journey of inner healing needed to remove those buttons. When identifying an emotion, measure it by rating how much you feel that emotion on a scale of 0-10 (0 = not feeling it at all and 10 = feeling it the most). Next, you can explore different avenues to help decrease the rating of the negative emotion.

For instance, if you feel abandoned by a loved one to a point of 6 on the scale, a good starting goal would be to lower the rating down to 3, and then ultimately to 0. You can spend time alone with God in His Word and prayer, as well as invest in *other* loving relationships to accomplish your goal. By remembering that God will never leave you and that other people love you, your feelings of abandonment will decrease on the scale. This is a good time to seek God for His peace-giving perspective. When you reach 0 on the scale, it is a good idea to say a prayer breaking agreement with the negative emotion and making agreement with God's perspective. (Chapters five and six will explain breaking agreements in greater detail.) Other negative emotions can be addressed in the same manner. During this stage, many people need to seek help with a trusted prayer partner, minister, and/or professional counselor. Please heed the advice of Proverbs 11:14: "Where there is no counsel, the people fall; But in the multitude of counselors there is safety."

Once you meet goals of working through emotions, you can then set goals for the relationship. Quality time, healthy communication, and increased empathy are just a few examples of goals that can help improve relations. If you are in a difficult relationship, I encourage you to discuss the possibility of setting goals with the other person. If he/she is not favorable to the idea of setting goals, continue setting personal goals and see how God can use your transformation to improve the relationship. When you do, it is possible that you will influence the other person to want to change as well.

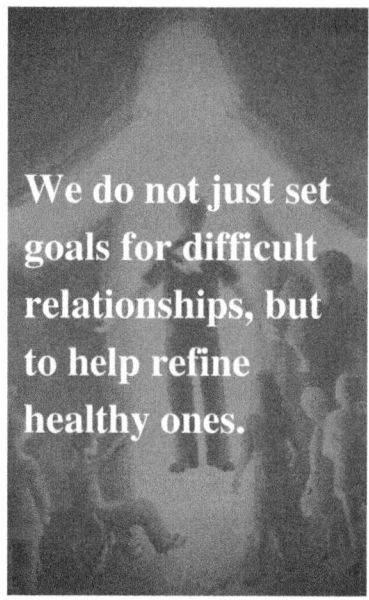

We do not just set goals for difficult relationships, but to help refine healthy ones. Strengthening an already strong bond between two individuals can lessen the possibility of misunderstandings that surface in *any* relationship. Seek God to show you His plans for the relationship, and He will lead the two of you in setting goals. As these goals are delineated into smaller, attainable steps, the relationship will be founded on a hope that replaces defeat.

Hope

> "For I know the plans I have for you," says the LORD. "They are plans for good and not for disaster, to give you a future and a hope."
>
> —JEREMIAH 29:11 (NLT)

While many people can quote Jeremiah 29:11, most people do not realize the context in which the verse was written. God was speaking through Jeremiah to the Israelites, who were taken captive to Babylon.[7] Not only were they in exile, but the Bible says that God caused them to be taken captive. It is hard to grasp that God, who brings abundant life, would allow His children to be taken captive. However, God provided a way for them to have peace, even in captivity. He tells them to continue living life as normal and to seek Him to bring peace into their place of captivity.

> *Build houses and dwell in them; plant gardens and eat their fruit. Take wives and beget sons and daughters; and take wives for your sons and give your daughters to husbands, so that they may bear sons and daughters—that you may be increased there, and not diminished. And seek the peace of the city where I have caused you to be carried away captive, and pray to the Lord for it; for in its peace you will have peace.*
>
> *— Jeremiah 29:5-7*

If you are one of the many people who feels captive in your own home, I encourage you to seek God for peace there. Contrary to what you see, your situation is not hopeless; God can bring peace to your place of exile. Hang on and see Jeremiah 29:11 come to pass! (Note: The exception to this is if you are in an unsafe place; know that abuse is not OK and that God may be removing you from the situation for your safety.) If you continually focus on your bondage, your perspective will steal your hope. Proverbs 13:12 tells us, "Hope deferred makes the heart sick." It is imperative that we allow hope to rise within us if we want to see seemingly hopeless relationships restored and refined. Imagine your hands grasping on to all the pain from a hopeless relationship. Now, imagine hope entering and your fingers loosening off of the pain one finger at a time. You are still holding the pain, but hope positions you to let God take it. Your hands are then open and ready to receive what God has for you in place of all the pain you were previously holding.

I love how Paul wrote eloquently to the church at Ephesus

about the importance of a perspective that produces hope. In Ephesians 1:17-19, he told them he was praying:

> *that the God of our Lord Jesus Christ, the Father of glory, may give to you the spirit of wisdom and revelation in the knowledge of Him, <u>the eyes of your understanding being enlightened; that you may know what is the hope of His calling,</u> what are the riches of the glory of His inheritance in the saints, and what is the exceeding greatness of His power toward us who believe, according to the working of His mighty power[.]* (EMPHASIS ADDED)

How do we attain the hope that we need to persevere through tough times with others? I believe true overcoming hope is birthed by receiving God's unconditional love for us.

According to 1 Corinthians 13:13, "...now abide faith, hope, love, these three; but the greatest of these is love." When we receive God's foundational love, we experience everlasting hope from which faith arises. Hebrews 11:1 tells us: *"Now faith is the substance of things hoped for, the evidence of things not seen."* Because of hope, we have faith to believe God's promise that He causes all things to work out for us.[8] I like to think of it like a three-tiered wedding cake, as in Figure 1-3:

Figure 1-3

Have you noticed hope depleting in your life and relationships? Receiving the incredible love of God is the answer to your hopelessness. When we receive the unending, life-changing love of God, hope will automatically grow within us and position us to have the faith needed to see transformation. We will then be more willing to apply the discipline needed to achieve our goals, and we will enjoy each step along the way in the journey to victory.

Discipline

> *All athletes are disciplined in their training. They do it to win a prize that will fade away, but we do it for an eternal prize.*
>
> — *1 Corinthians 9:25 (NLT)*

Every achievement requires work, which, in turn, requires discipline. Personally, I have played trumpet since I was in the sixth grade and have found that reaching a high level of proficiency requires great sacrifice. Throughout the years, commitment to my goal often included doing things I did not enjoy. I remember countless times even dreading practice time, but once I got started it was not so bad; as I improved and could play more difficult pieces, I actually started enjoying practicing. If I did not have the discipline to work through times of intense practice sessions, I would not have had the joy of performing incredible compositions with a symphonic band or orchestra.

Maybe you are not a musician and you do not have any reference for understanding the discipline it takes to master a musical instrument. If so, think about an athlete; she trains to win a prize that will fade away, but we train for an eternal prize. Each athlete that enters the stadium at the opening ceremonies of the

Olympics represents countless hours of disciplined training and untold dollars spent on coaches and equipment. I can only imagine the sense of accomplishment and satisfaction that arises in their spirits even to represent their countries in the opening ceremonies, let alone to make it to the medal stand. If athletes can invest all of that hard work into a temporal Olympic medal, how much more should we discipline ourselves to work toward reconciling relationships with people who will be in Heaven with us! As the author of Hebrews exhorts,

 *So do not throw away this confident trust in the Lord. Remember the great reward it brings you! Patient endurance is what you need now, so that you will continue to do God's will. Then you will receive all that he has promised.*

— HEBREWS 10:35-36 (NLT)

God lays out guidelines in His Word that will help us live a peaceful life with others. When we do not discipline ourselves to heed those instructions, we then encounter discipline from our Heavenly Father. Thinking back over my own life, it seems that most of the discipline I have experienced from God was directly related to how I interact with others, not unlike a parent who disciplines his children when they argue with each other.

 My son, do not despise the Lord's discipline, and do not resent his rebuke, because the Lord disciplines those he loves, as a father the son he delights in.

— PROVERBS 3:11-12 (NIV)

After quoting this passage from Proverbs, the author of Hebrews writes,

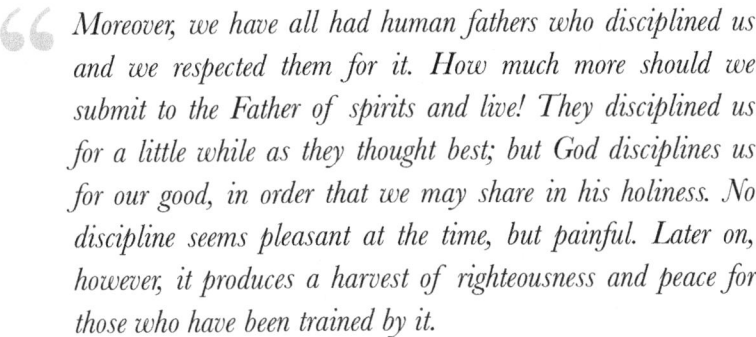

Moreover, we have all had human fathers who disciplined us and we respected them for it. How much more should we submit to the Father of spirits and live! They disciplined us for a little while as they thought best; but God disciplines us for our good, in order that we may share in his holiness. No discipline seems pleasant at the time, but painful. Later on, however, it produces a harvest of righteousness and peace for those who have been trained by it.

— *Hebrews 12:9-11 (NIV)*

I love how this passage says that discipline produces "a harvest of righteousness and peace." As we follow God's guidelines and accept His correction, we will begin to activate the righteousness He gave us when we accepted Christ's death and resurrection.[9] As we make right choices and live righteous lives, we will begin to see more peace within our relationships.

Sometimes it is not possible to have peace with another person. Romans 12:18 says, "If it is possible, as much as depends on you, live peaceably with all men." If is it not possible to have peace with the other person, you can still have peace within your own soul and trust God to deal with her. However, sometimes I think we use Romans 12:18 as an excuse not to exert measurable effort on our side of the relationship. Maybe we do not try to mend broken relationships because we sincerely do not know what to do; if so, we need to discipline ourselves to seek God for a renewal of His wisdom. I love what James says about this:

But the wisdom that is from above is first pure, then peaceable, gentle, willing to yield, full of mercy and good fruits, without partiality and without hypocrisy. Now the fruit of righteousness is sown in peace by those who make peace.

– *James 3:17-18*

I am amazed to see how many scriptures in the Bible link wisdom and righteousness to our interactions with people. Notice how James writes in the verse above that wisdom breeds actions of peace, gentleness, and even a willingness to yield. In another passage, Paul prays for believers in Philippi to be filled with the fruits of righteousness and exhorts them to be without offense. I, too, pray the following prayer for you as Paul did:

> *And this I pray, that your love may abound still more and more in knowledge and all discernment, that you may approve the things that are excellent, that you may be sincere and without offense till the day of Christ, being filled with the fruits of righteousness which are by Jesus Christ, to the glory and praise of God.*
>
> — *PHILIPPIANS 1:9-11*

Remember, setting goals and remaining hopeful require discipline, and it is worth the effort! Countless marriage counselors, pastors, and teachers agree that it takes work to maintain a healthy relationship. Without discipline, our goals and hope are simply good intentions that never come to pass. However, applying self-discipline and allowing God's discipline will yield success and reason to thank God in celebration!

Celebrate!

> *But without faith it is impossible to please Him, for he who comes to God must believe that He is, and that <u>He is a rewarder of those who diligently seek Him</u>*
>
> — *HEBREWS 11:6 (EMPHASIS ADDED)*

The Bible reveals that God rewards a life of discipline. If God *wants* to reward us, we should be able to celebrate each time a goal is met. This celebrating is more about thanking God for what He has accomplished in and through us than it is about taking credit for ourselves. Romans 11:36 reminds us of this truth: "For of Him and through Him and to Him are all things, to whom be glory forever. Amen." All glory goes to God!

Sometimes celebration comes in the form of exuberant shouts of joy; other times it comes in quiet contentment and meditation on God's faithfulness to us through seasons of conflict. Paul must have experienced both joy and contentment in order to write what he wrote to the church in Phillippi:

> *Rejoice in the Lord always. Again I will say, rejoice!...I have learned in whatever state I am, to be content: I know how to be abased, and I know how to abound. Everywhere and in all things I have learned both to be full and to be hungry, both to abound and to suffer need. I can do all things through Christ who strengthens me.*
>
> — *Philippians 4:4, 11b-13*

How could Paul say that? The only way Paul could be joyful and content in whatever circumstance is by allowing God to give him a fresh perspective about what he was facing on any given day. Thus, he could have a deep satisfaction even in hard times, and he could have a humble gratitude in great times. I encourage you to reread the verse above with these words: "I have learned in whatever role I play, whether mother/father, sister/brother, daughter/son, spouse, friend, boss, employee, neighbor, etc, to be content." We can learn contentment in every relationship as we seek God to help us set goals, allow hope to arise, be disciplined to put the work into relationships, and celebrate each small step along the way.

Distractions

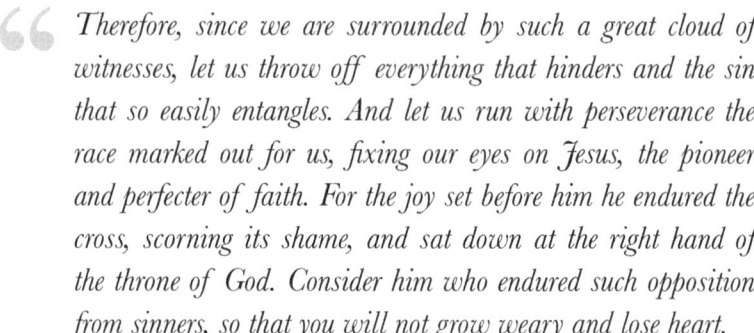

Therefore, since we are surrounded by such a great cloud of witnesses, let us throw off everything that hinders and the sin that so easily entangles. And let us run with perseverance the race marked out for us, fixing our eyes on Jesus, the pioneer and perfecter of faith. For the joy set before him he endured the cross, scorning its shame, and sat down at the right hand of the throne of God. Consider him who endured such opposition from sinners, so that you will not grow weary and lose heart.

— Hebrews 12:1-3 (NIV)

It is imperative for us to keep our eyes on the goal and not allow distractions to steal our attention. There are quite a few verses in the Old Testament that encourage us not to look to the left or the right. Most of these passages are referring to keeping the commandments, as referenced in Joshua 1:

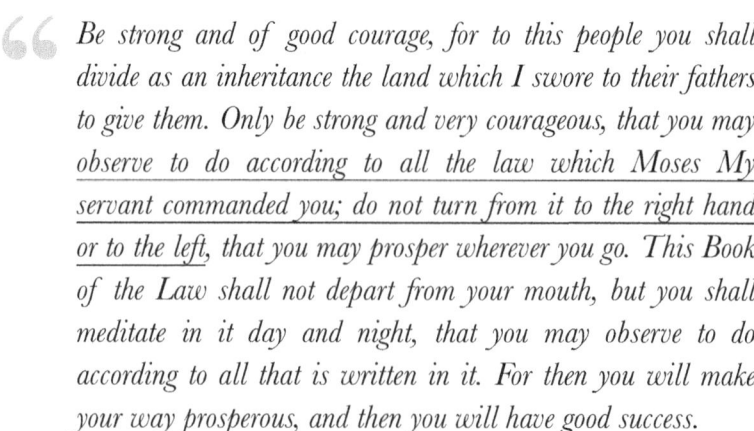

Be strong and of good courage, for to this people you shall divide as an inheritance the land which I swore to their fathers to give them. Only be strong and very courageous, that you may observe to do according to all the law which Moses My servant commanded you; do not turn from it to the right hand or to the left, that you may prosper wherever you go. This Book of the Law shall not depart from your mouth, but you shall meditate in it day and night, that you may observe to do according to all that is written in it. For then you will make your way prosperous, and then you will have good success.

— *JOSHUA 1:6-7 (EMPHASIS ADDED)*

One day, one of the religious leaders questioned Jesus about which was the greatest commandment in the law. The book of Matthew records his answer in chapter 22, verses 37-40:

> *Jesus said to him, "'You shall love the LORD your God with all your heart, with all your soul, and with all your mind.' This is the first and great commandment. And the second is like it: 'You shall love your neighbor as yourself.' On these two commandments hang all the Law and the Prophets."*

Jesus summarized all the Ten Commandments with two commandments which deal with relationships. From these verses, we see that the most important relationship we can have is with God Himself. The next relationship we need to refine is with self, since Jesus commanded us to "love your neighbor as yourself." After all, how can we show love to others if we do not extend love to ourselves? Finally, our relationships with others will be refined as they see Christ's

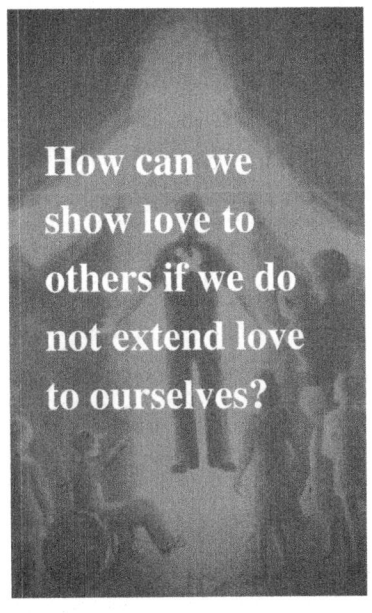

How can we show love to others if we do not extend love to ourselves?

character in us. When we put God's relationship first, He will heal our personal inner wounds and help us relate to others better. No wonder the enemy, also known as Satan,[10] the devil,[11] the father of all lies,[12] and the accuser,[13] tries everything in his power to destroy relationships!

There will be plenty of opportunities for you to be distracted with things on the left and on the right that will remove your focus from the two greatest commandments. As you continue reading this book, I challenge you to take a mental note of what distracts you. People will say and do things that the enemy uses like bait to offend and distract you; each time this happens, surrender it to the Lord quickly. For example, you may care about what people think more than what God thinks, or you may desire to control the situation; remember, you must seek God for His perspective and let go of your own perspective when these things happen.

In this day and age, the temptation to log into social media or check for texts and emails is a huge relationship buster! Next time you go to a restaurant, look around and see how many people have their heads bowed—not to pray over their meal, but to be mesmerized by their smartphones. Many of them have earbuds in so that they can listen to music or the latest video, rather than intentionally hearing what is on the heart of the person across the table. How sad that the dinner table, the place of fellowship and family bonding, has become a place where families drift further apart into their own technology worlds.

Obviously, the rise of pornography addictions, due to easy access in the palm of a hand, also causes destruction in relationships of every level. However, even screen time that is seemingly harmless can come between individuals, keeping them from meaningful connections. I encourage you to put your devices down and show your loved ones that you value time with them more than time on your phone or tablet. If you cannot do without technology for 30 minutes at the dinner table, you may need to get help to conquer your addiction.

Sometimes we say we value relationships, but our actions do not reflect our claim. Nothing is impossible! Even technology addictions can be conquered when we ask God to intervene. Ask

Him to restore your passion for a love for Him, and then for yourself and others. I am praying for you as you start a journey to refine relationships.

Prayer

Lord, I look to You, the pioneer and perfecter of my faith, to help me as I seek Your perspective. Show me where my skewed perceptions have caused misunderstandings and dysfunctional relationships. I offer up the hurts and wounds that keep me from experiencing Your blood-bought freedom. Please soften my heart to the material presented in this book that will help me in the journey to refining my relationships. I pray for healthy relationships in my life to reflect Your glory and for unhealthy relationships to be transformed. In Jesus' Name, Amen!

2

REFINING A RELATIONSHIP WITH GOD

> ❝ *My beloved spoke, and said to me: "Rise up, my love, my fair one, And come away."*
>
> — *SONG OF SOLOMON 2:10*

> ❝ *"Behold, I stand at the door and knock. If anyone hears My voice and opens the door, I will come in to him and dine with him, and he with Me."*
>
> — *REVELATION 3:20*

WHAT A WONDER to think that God, the Creator of the universe, pursues me to have an intimate relationship with Him! Many people do not even think about God in their lives, let alone a relationship with Him. Even some people who identify as Christians miss out on experiencing a close connection with the Lord. Although many people have put their faith in Jesus to save them from their sins, how many have a friendship with Him? The verse Revelation 3:20, written at the beginning of this chapter, is often quoted in order to help a lost person become a Christian. However, this verse was originally written to believers. It is an invitation to let Christ come in and be a friend, much like friends share dinner together. In John 15:15, Jesus said, "No longer do I call you servants, for a servant does not know what his master is doing; but I have called you friends, for all things that I heard from My Father I have made known to you."

Sadly, many people go to church regularly and learn about God, but they still do not know God. When my girls were in elementary school, George W. Bush was the president of the United States. One day I asked them, "Do you know George Bush?"

Both of them responded enthusiastically, "Yes, we know George Bush!"

"You do? You know George Bush?"

"Yes, Mom! He is the president of the United States; of course we know George Bush!"

"When did you meet him?"

Their enthusiasm melted into confusion as their eyes seemed to say, "huh?"

I said, "I think you know *about* George Bush, but you have never met him personally and had a relationship with him." I proceeded to tell them that many people think they know God, but until they meet Jesus and have a personal relationship with Him, they do not truly *know* Him.

The Bible says that we are all sinners and the wages of our sin is death.[1] Our wrongdoings, ranging from "little white lies" all the way to murder, separate us from God. However, God, in His infinite love and mercy, made a way for us to be reconciled to Him by placing all of our sins on Jesus, who never sinned, and by letting Jesus pay for our sins when He was crucified on a cross.[2] Jesus left His throne in Heaven to take on human form through a virgin birth and die so that we may have eternal life. He was both fully God and fully man. Jesus' divinity is imperative because if He was just another sinful man, how could His death benefit us? The fact that He was a man is also imperative because a man was required in order to pay the price for the sins of mankind. Not only did Jesus die on our behalf, but He also rose from the dead and is alive today.[3] No wonder Luke wrote that there is no other way to salvation except through Jesus.[4] All we have to do is acknowledge our wrongdoings which separate us from God, thank Jesus for taking our punishment, and ask Him to come into our lives to begin a friendship with us. (For further explanation on this, see the appendix in the back of the book.)

God's Love For Us

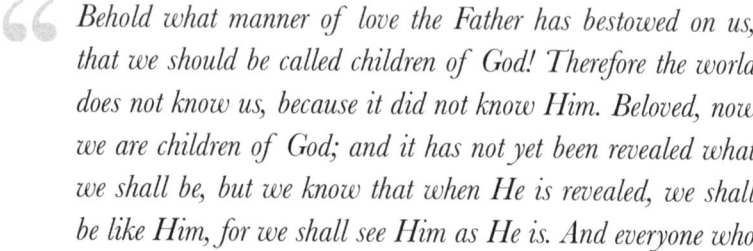

Behold what manner of love the Father has bestowed on us, that we should be called children of God! Therefore the world does not know us, because it did not know Him. Beloved, now we are children of God; and it has not yet been revealed what we shall be, but we know that when He is revealed, we shall be like Him, for we shall see Him as He is. And everyone who has this hope in Him purifies himself, just as He is pure.

— *1 JOHN 3:1-3*

Our relationship with God is not just about us receiving Him into our lives and loving Him, but it has everything to do with how much He loves us! He did not just create us and leave us to live our lives the best we can. We know that God the Father loves us so much that He sent His Son to pay the price for our sins.[5] We also know that we are Jesus' joy and the reason He endured the cross.[6] After Jesus' death and resurrection, God lovingly sent us the Holy Spirit to dwell within us and be our helper, teacher, and guide on our journey here on earth.[7] Finally, God's ultimate desire for us is to be with Him forever in Heaven after we die. This divine love that started before we were born continues throughout eternity in Heaven and gives us a deep hope that actually purifies us!

The Bible calls the Church the Bride of Christ. I remember how I felt when my husband first started pursuing me. I felt valued, and I longed to be with him, especially leading up to the wedding day. We both wanted to spend time getting to know each other better. Similarly, God pursues us and longs to be with us; however, He already knows us better than we know ourselves. Even so, He longs for us to be with Him so that we may get to know Him better. He does not expect us to perform in order to earn His love—He already loves us! There is nothing we can do to make Him love us more. Likewise, there is nothing we can do to make Him love us less. When we respond to His loving pursuit of us, we will find that in His presence is fullness of joy.[8] Though we will face adversity as long as we live on the earth, He has promised to be with us and give us His peace in the midst of trials.[9]

Our Love For God

 We love Him because He first loved us.

— *1 John 4:19*

When we get to know God, we will experience how much He truly loves us. His love for us prompts a desire in us to love Him back.[10] Jesus said that we should love Him with all of our heart.[11] The Greek word for "heart" is *kardia.* According to *Blue Letter Bible*, besides meaning the organ in the body that pumps blood, it also refers to:

1. The center and seat of spiritual life

- The soul or mind, as it is the fountain and seat of the thoughts, passions, desires, appetites, affections, purposes, endeavors
- Of the understanding, the faculty and seat of the intelligence
- Of the will and character
- Of the soul so far as it is affected and stirred in a bad way or good, or of the soul as the seat of the sensibilities, affections, emotions, desires, appetites, passions

2. Of the middle or central or inmost part of anything[12]

When I first read this definition of *kardia,* I was amazed to learn all of the areas that *kardia* encompasses. God is asking us to love Him with our desires, appetites, intellect, and the inmost part of our souls. The only way we can love Him completely is to let Him be the Lord of our lives. We cannot prioritize God only from 10:00 AM to noon on Sundays and five to ten minutes a day (if that) for devotionals. He wants to be the center of our lives 24 hours a day, just like Moses mentioned in Deuteronomy 6:6-7:

 And these words which I command you today shall be in your

heart. You shall teach them diligently to your children, and shall talk of them when you sit in your house, when you walk by the way, when you lie down, and when you rise up.

The Ripple Effect of God's Love

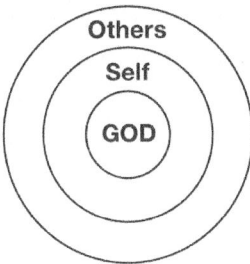

Figure 2-1

When a rock is thrown into a pond, it creates a small, circular ripple that continues expanding outward. This is known as a "ripple effect." Our relationships operate similarly (See Figure 2-1). If we cultivate an intimate relationship with God in our spirits, the inner core of our beings, the ripple effects will be healthy. Our relationship with God will help heal our inner wounds and help us have a healthy relationship with ourselves. Then we will be able to build thriving relationships with others because we will not be dependent on them to make us happy.

We read in 1 Peter 5:7 (NLT), "Give all your worries and cares to God, for he cares about you." God truly loves and cares about us! What concerns us concerns Him, and most of what concerns us deals with other people. Unfortunately, we often focus on problems we have with other people without even consulting the Lord. When we fail to seek God first, we veer off track by placing relationships with others before our relationship with God. When we put God first, He will bring healthy function to our lives and show us how to love ourselves and others according to His ultimate plan and purpose.

Self-Assessment of My Relationship with God

In order to evaluate your relationship with God, I have created a self-assessment at the end of the chapter. Rate each statement according to how often each one feels true:

Never | Rarely | Sometimes | Often | Always

When scoring yourself, please be honest. No one else will see your answers unless you share them.

1. I enjoy spending time alone with God

Before you rate yourself on this statement, be honest and think about how much time you actually spend with God. God is always with us, but we are often not aware of His presence. We let the busyness of everyday life crowd out spending time with God instead of intentionally pursuing Him. The days I start by spending time with God are much more meaningful than the days when I wake up late and rush out the door. I also sleep better if I take time at the end of each day to surrender everything that happened to God. These intentional meetings alone with God increase my awareness of His presence throughout the day.

Some people struggle with knowing how to spend time with God. We can read the Bible, pray, and worship, but we can also sit still and enjoy His company. Setting aside a special place to be with God, whether it be a prayer closet or simply a prayer chair, helps to lessen distractions. It is a good idea to have things you need close by, like a Bible, journal, and a pen. It is also a good idea *not* to have some things there, like your phone or computer, unless you use them for worship music or reading the Bible. For anyone who thinks he does not have a place he can go to, consider the life of Susanna Wesley, mother of John and Charles Wesley:

> One of the most dramatic examples of how busy and crowded the house often was is that as a signal to her children to be quiet, Susanna would sometimes sit down and pull her apron over her head so that she could pray in peace. When she was [in this position], the children knew not to interrupt her.[13]

2. I love to read and meditate on the Word of God.

Psalm 119 is the longest chapter in the Bible. Its theme focuses on the benefits of God's Word to us. Here are just a few of the verses from Psalm 119 about the advantages of applying the Bible to our lives:

> *Your word I have hidden in my heart,*
> *That I might not sin against You.*
>
> — *PSALM 119:11*

> *Let Your mercies come also to me, O Lord*
> *Your salvation according to Your word.*
> *So shall I have an answer for him who reproaches me,*
> *For I trust in Your word.*
>
> — *PSALM 119:41-42*

> *Forever, O Lord, Your word is settled in heaven.*
>
> — PSALM 119:89

> *Unless Your law had been my delight,*
>   *I would then have perished in my affliction.*
> *I will never forget Your precepts,*
>   *For by them You have given me life.*
>
> — PSALM 119:92-93

> *How sweet are Your words to my taste,*
>   *Sweeter than honey to my mouth!*
> *Through Your precepts I get understanding;*
>   *Therefore I hate every false way.*
> *Your word is a lamp to my feet*
>   *And a light to my path.*
>
> — PSALM 119:103-105

What a blessing to have the written Word of God to guide us in life. Just like we starve our physical bodies when we do not eat, we also starve our spirits when we neglect to read and meditate on God's Word. We are not condemned if we do not read the Bible; rather, we are blessed so much if we do! If you do not know where to start, I suggest that you start by reading the book of John in the New Testament to learn more about Jesus. Alternatively, you can also find a single verse that speaks to you, such as the verses listed above, and meditate on what God is saying to you through that verse.

3. In prayer, I take time to listen to God and not just be the one talking all the time.

Many Christians miss out on intimate times with God because they do not believe that He still speaks to us. There is a type of prayer called "listening prayer" where we ask God questions and listen for Him to respond. The book of John speaks of Jesus as being our Good Shepherd.[14] He said that His sheep recognize His voice.[15] God speaks in many ways, including through the Bible, through circumstances, and through His still, small voice in our spirits. It is fine to question God, but we need to listen for His answer. Sometimes He will respond quickly in our spirits, and other times His answer comes later. If you sense that God may be answering, but you do not know if it is indeed God, ask yourself, "Would the enemy have told me this? Does what I think I heard contradict with the Bible?" If the answer to each question is "no," then it is probably the voice of the Holy Spirit. Yes, sometimes the devil will come disguised as an angel of light, but God will expose the schemes of the enemy. If God does not answer quickly, then pray that your spiritual ears will be opened to hear when the answer comes.

4. I share my faith in Jesus with other people.

Revival Outside the Walls is an organization that encourages believers to share their faith with unchurched people. On their website I found many statistics from various reputable sources. It saddened me to find out just how uninvolved most Christians are in sharing the Good News. For instance:

- 70% of those attending church one or more times a month never share their faith with a stranger.[16]

- 70% unchurched people have never been invited to church in their whole lives.[17]
- Only 2% of churchgoers invited an unchurched person to church in the last year.[18]
- 80% of unchurched people are open to the gospel.[19]
- 71% of the unchurched say they are likely to accept a personal invitation from a family member, friend, or neighbor to attend church.[20]
- 50% of churchgoers are unsure if people who know them are aware that they are Christians.[21]

> When we spend time alone with God, our hearts become full and we will want to follow Jesus' instructions to take the Gospel to others.

Why do most Christians not share their faith with others? I am sure there are many reasons, but the main contributing factor is our lack of spending time with God. When we spend time alone with God, our hearts become full and we will want to follow Jesus' instructions to take the Gospel to others.[22] We also may not share our faith because we are afraid of what people will think. I do not want to be ashamed of Jesus. Instead, I agree with what Paul wrote in Romans 1:16: "For I am not ashamed of the gospel of Christ, for it is the power of God to salvation for everyone who believes."[23] There is no greater satisfaction than the joy that comes when God opens the door for me to introduce someone to Him. Not only am I excited about the possibility of someone spending eternity with Jesus in Heaven, but I am also glad when she can experience the abundant life on earth that new life in Christ brings.

5. I consciously make an effort to thank God for His faithfulness in my life.

Living a life of gratitude reaps great rewards. Even secular research studies have found that people who are grateful experience better health physically, mentally, and emotionally.[24] If people who do not know God experience these benefits, how much more do believers benefit when they thank God, the Creator of all, on a daily basis?

Think about how much thanking loved ones strengthens our relationships with them. When we thank others, we demonstrate how much we value them in our lives. Likewise, when we thank God, we demonstrate how much we value Him in our lives. If you can't think of something to thank God for, remember that His mercies are new every morning. Thank Him for new beginnings when you wake up each day. Many people want to know God's will; being thankful is God's will!

> *Be thankful in all circumstances, for this is God's will for you who belong to Christ Jesus.*
>
> — *1 Thessalonians 5:18 (NLT)*

6. I cheerfully give of my finances to support God's work.

> *Will a man rob God? Yet you have robbed Me!*
> *But you say,*
> *'In what way have we robbed You?'*
> *In tithes and offerings.*
> *Bring all the tithes into the storehouse,*
> *That there may be food in My house,*
> *And try Me now in this,"*

Says the Lord of hosts,
"If I will not open for you the windows of heaven
And pour out for you such blessing
That there will not be room enough to receive it.

— *MALACHI 3:8, 10*

Giving tithes and offerings to God for His work is an act of faith. Some people say that tithing is of the Old Testament Law and thus does not apply today. However, the act of tithing ten percent of income was first done by Abraham to Melchizedek many years before God gave the Ten Commandments to Moses.[25] Sacrifice in the area of finances is a way to show God how much we value Him. It is also a way we can partner with God in advancing His Kingdom. There is a blessing that comes with sacrificial giving. When we give sacrificially, we find out that God can do more with the ninety percent than we could ever do with one hundred percent of our finances.

7. I feel obligated to read the Bible and pray.

At first glance, this statement might seem like a positive statement. It is true that reading the Bible and praying are necessary to develop an intimate relationship with God. However, reading the Bible and praying from a sense of obligation, rather than from a longing to be with Him, propels us into a rut of religious activity instead of into an intimate relationship with God. If we merely read the Word and pray because we think we have to, then we are being led by our flesh and will fall into the trap of false guilt and condemnation. However, freedom comes when we follow God's promptings in our spirit to read the Word and pray. Sometimes you may be led of the Holy Spirit to read a whole book in the Bible, and other times God will have you meditate on one verse. When you follow His lead and feast on His Word, you will automatically respond with prayer and worship, and you will understand what it means to walk according to the Spirit.

 There is therefore now no condemnation to those who are in Christ Jesus, who do not walk according to the flesh, but according to the Spirit.

— ROMANS 8:1

8. I tend to look to others to meet my needs instead of totally relying on God.

Matthew 6:25-34 records a portion of Jesus' incredible Sermon on the Mount in which Jesus encourages us not to worry about the fulfillment of our needs. He admonishes us not to be concerned, stating, "[Y]our heavenly Father knows that you need all these things. But seek first the kingdom of God and His righteousness, and all these things shall be added to you."[26]

God may actually use others as vessels to meet our needs, but He is ultimately our source. Romans 12:6-8 outlines a set of gifts, often labeled "Motivational Gifts," which God develops within believers in order to meet our collective needs. God's plan for the Church is a functional environment where people with diverse giftings edify one another. It is a beautiful plan set into motion by our Creator to meet our needs through each other, including spiritual, financial, and organizational needs, among others. However, when we focus on the people God uses to reach out to us instead of on Him as our ultimate source, we will be disappointed. As will be discussed in chapter six of this book, disappointment comes when people do not meet our expectations, but we also disappoint them when we fail to meet their expectations. Our hope lies in God, the only One who will never let us down.[27]

9. I tend to blame God for trials in my life.

> *"For My thoughts are not your thoughts,*
>   *Nor are your ways My ways," says the LORD.*
>   *"For as the heavens are higher than the earth,*
>   *So are My ways higher than your ways,*
>   *And My thoughts than your thoughts."*

— ISAIAH 55:8-9

> *He causes his sun to rise on the evil and the good, and sends*
> *rain on the righteous and the unrighteous.*

— MATTHEW 5:45B (NIV)

Jesus warned us that we would face trials and tribulations on this earth. The good news is that He has overcome the world; thus, if we surrender our lives to Him, we will overcome every adversity that comes our way. It is hard to believe that God will use adversity for our good when we are in the midst of a storm. During tumultuous times, we need the "peace that passes all understanding" that only Jesus, the Prince of Peace, can give.[28] Rather than blaming God for trials in our lives, we need to ask Him what He wants us to learn during these seasons. When we look back over our lives, we will find that our faith was strengthened more during hard times than during times of comfort.

> *In this you greatly rejoice, though now for a little while, if*
> *need be, you have been grieved by various trials, that the*
> *genuineness of your faith, being much more precious than gold*
> *that perishes, though it is tested by fire, may be found to praise,*
> *honor, and glory at the revelation of Jesus Christ, whom*

having not seen you love. Though now you do not see Him, yet believing, you rejoice with joy inexpressible and full of glory, receiving the end of your faith—the salvation of your souls.

— *1 Peter 1:6-9*

10. I have a hard time trusting God.

Though some people do not blame God for trials in their lives, they still have a hard time trusting Him to take care of them. Perhaps other people have let them down and they are projecting their issues with other people onto God. This is especially true if a person's parents, who were supposed to nurture and care for them, failed them. I love what the New Living Translation says in Psalm 27:10: "Even if my father and mother abandon me, the Lord will hold me close."

We may have a hard time trusting people after they fail us, especially if we have been betrayed by loved ones. As will be discussed in chapter five, when loved ones betray us, we need to release and forgive them and then place our trust in God. Though easier said than done, as we allow God's unconditional love and forgiveness to flow through us, we will start to trust God more.

 Trust in the Lord with all your heart,
And lean not on your own understanding;
In all your ways acknowledge Him,
And He shall direct your paths.

— *Proverbs 3:5-6*

11. When facing a difficult time, I tend to forget that God is with me and that I can call on Him.

Many people believe in a "higher being" but do not realize that God wants to be involved in their lives on a personal basis. These people do not even have a framework in place from which to call out to God. As Christians, we say that our faith is not about religion as much as it is about a relationship with Jesus, yet, sadly, many Christians still do not commune with God regularly. We forget that God wants us to give all of our concerns to Him.[29] He not only cares about us, but He cares about what we care about. Psalm 138:8 says, "The Lord will perfect that which concerns me."

Like most people, I used to be quick to call a friend when I was facing a trial and would rehash all my concerns. I have learned over the years to consult God first. After praying about the situation, I sometimes realize that I no longer need to call my friend because I have released my burdens to the Lord. I wonder if there have been times when my trial lingered because I did not seek God first. James 4:2b (NIV) says, "You do not have because you do not ask God." God challenges us to call on Him and let Him do great and mighty things in our lives.

> *Call to Me, and I will answer you, and show you great and mighty things, which you do not know.*
>
> —*JEREMIAH 33:3*

12. I have a difficult time engaging my heart in worship.

I have a friend who went to Bible college and was involved in the chapel worship team. She said that one time she was singing, lifting her hands, and even dancing around during the worship time when she heard the Holy Spirit say to her spirit, "You are not even thinking about Me right now." Wow! I often think about that story and check to see if I am engaging my heart in true worship.

As was mentioned earlier in this chapter, true worship encompasses more than just our outward actions; it involves our heart, the inner core of who we are. Worship extends beyond the congregational singing that precedes a pastor's message. I love to praise God in song, but music itself is not worship. The physical act of singing or raising hands should be an automatic response to an inner, heart-felt adoration of God.

We cannot create worship; true worship begins and ends with God. When we realize that God extends His love to us, we encounter Him in a special way and express our love back to Him. We can experience freedom in worship all day long in everything we do. What a difference it would make if we all realized that our outward actions can be a reflection of true worship!

 But the hour is coming, and now is, when the true worshipers will worship the Father in spirit and truth; for the Father is seeking such to worship Him. God is Spirit, and those who worship Him must worship in spirit and truth.

— JOHN 4:23-24

Self-Assessment Statements for Relationship with God	How often is the statement true? 1 - never 5 - always				
1. I enjoy spending time alone with God.	1	2	3	4	5
2. I take pleasure in reading and meditating on the Word of God.	1	2	3	4	5
3. In prayer, I take time to listen to God and not just be the one talking all the time.	1	2	3	4	5
4. I share my faith in Jesus with other people.	1	2	3	4	5
5. I consciously make an effort to thank God for His faithfulness in my life.	1	2	3	4	5
6. I cheerfully give of my finances to support God's work.	1	2	3	4	5
7. I feel obligated to read the Bible and pray.	1	2	3	4	5
8. I look to others to meet my needs instead of totally relying on God.	1	2	3	4	5
9. I blame God for trials in my life.	1	2	3	4	5
10. I have a hard time trusting God.	1	2	3	4	5
11. When facing a difficult time, I forget that God is with me and that I can call on Him.	1	2	3	4	5
12. I have a hard time engaging my heart in worship.	1	2	3	4	5

To find your score, take the total scores of statements 1 through 6 and subtract the total scores of statements 7 through 12.

Total score of statements 1-6: _____
Total score of statements 7-12: _____
Final Score: _____

Your assessment score will be compared to the process of gold being refined. The first step is to mine for gold in its raw form. The gold is then put through fire and melted in order to let the impurities rise to the surface and be skimmed off. The process continues until the last impurity is purged and the master refiner sees his image when he looks into the fine medal.

If your score falls between -24 and -8, your ground is ready to be mined for gold! The fact that you are reading this book and have taken time to assess your relationship with God shows that you are contemplating developing a relationship with Him. Congratulations for making a decision to start the process of finding the gold and allowing God to refine the gold so that impurities can be removed.

If your score falls between -7 and 8, you are in the process of being refined by fire. Impurities have started being removed, but there are still a number of impurities yet to be purged. You are starting to realize that you can have a relationship with God that goes beyond your initial commitment to serve Him. However, the cares of this world may still be hindering you from having a daily, intimate relationship with God. You are likely facing some hard times as you allow God to purify you with fire. Remember that the pain of the refining process is small compared to the joy that results in intimacy with God.

If your score falls between 9 and 24, you have been through the fire and had many impurities removed. You have not only made a commitment to serve God, but you have encountered God at a deeper level. At this level of intimacy with God, you are in a position be warned so that you can avoid impurities rather than having to be purged of them. Keep seeking Him in order to maintain your relationship with Him and continue to let residue of impurities rise to the top.

REFINING A RELATIONSHIP WITH SELF

“ *Beloved, if our heart does not condemn us, we have confidence toward God.*

— *1 John 3:21*

G ROWING UP AS the daughter of a commercial airline pilot, I was blessed to have opportunities to travel. After traveling so frequently, I could almost recite the safety lecture given before takeoff. I was especially intrigued by the possibility of an emergency causing an oxygen mask to suddenly dangle in front of my face. I also pondered why the announcer warned parents to adjust their own oxygen masks before assisting young children. I now know that adults will be better positioned to help their children if they first obtain their own source of oxygen. In the same way, we have to refine the relationship with self before we can effectively build quality relationships with anyone else.

Some people may find it difficult to think about having a "relationship" with themselves. I am not talking about brewing myself two cups of coffee and sitting down to have a conversation with myself. I am certainly not talking about sologamy, the act of marrying one's self, which has actually become a new movement in the 21st century. Rather, I am talking about having peace within myself and my true identity in Christ. Think of it this way: I can get away from everyone else, including my spouse, but I can never get away from myself. When I go to bed, I am there. When I wake up, I am there. When I go to school, work, or the grocery store, I am there. With that in mind, it is imperative to get along with myself in order to live a satisfied life.

When we put Him first, He blesses us with rest.

As was previously mentioned in the first chapter, Jesus said that the greatest commandment is to love God, followed by loving others as we love ourselves.[1] These two commandments are so important that, according to Jesus, all the Law hangs on them.[2] Though the Ten Commandments clearly align with loving God and others, how do they show the importance of loving self? The fourth commandment to honor the Sabbath is where I believe God shows us the importance of taking care of ourselves. Honoring the Sabbath not only shows our love for God, but it also embraces love for self through self-care. When we put Him first, He blesses us with rest.

When I say that we need to refine our relationship with self before refining relationships with others, I am not saying we need to love ourselves *more* than we love others or to think of ourselves as *better* than others. Paul warns us not to think too highly of ourselves.[3] He proceeds to explain that we should honor others by giving them preference over ourselves.[4]

Removing Walls

Sadly, some people have so many unhealed wounds from their past that, consequently, they build up walls as a coping mechanism for "protection"; in reality, instead of being protected, their walls create a self-imposed emotional exile. It is then easy to fall into a self-absorption mode of being a victim, rather than being victorious. As a "victim," one thinks so much about his own negative circumstances that he is not aware of how God can work through his situation, nor does he value anyone else. He may even start hating others and himself because he will not have an accurate understanding of either one. Notice in Figure 3-1 that the brick wall is located between God and others. When we hide behind a wall, not only do we forfeit the Peace of God that already exists in us as believers, but we also hinder others from seeing Christ in us.

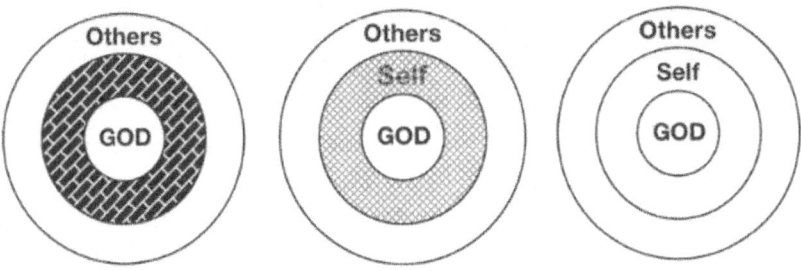

Figures 3-1 | 3-2 | 3-3

Figure 3-2 represents a healthier option of replacing any wall we erect with a filter of God's Word. When we filter others' actions and our thoughts towards them through His Word, we are positioned to trust God to heal us from all our inner wounds. The Bible has a response for anything we face in life. For example, if we feel lonely, God's Word tells us that He will never leave us.[5] If we are bitter about what someone did to us, God's Word urges us to forgive, just as Christ has forgiven us.[6] As we filter our thoughts with the Bible and let God heal our inner wounds, we will be equipped to remove the wall, as represented by Figure 3-3.

Figure 3-3 also represents the purity of a relationship with God shining through us. The reason there is a wall in Figure 3-1 is because of inner wounds. As we allow God to transform us, we will have more intimacy with Him, and others will be able to see His transforming work in our lives. We will also be positioned to develop healthy relationships with others.

Self-Assessment of My Relationship with Self

Like the self-assessment in chapter two, please rate the following statements according to how often each statement feels true. Remember to be honest when answering so that you may know what goals to set in your relationship with self.

1. I enjoy being by myself.

Some people are energized by being with others, while other people are refreshed more when they are alone. On the contrary, even extroverted people need to be at peace when they are alone. They may be alone, but they do not have to be lonely. When someone is alone, it merely means no one else is with her. However, loneliness carries a sadness that leads to despair. One person can be alone and be content, while someone else can be in a crowd, yet still be lonely.

Some people keep themselves busy in order to avoid the negative feelings they experience when they are alone. In art therapy, I sometimes have clients draw their face three times to illustrate the way they think people see them, the way they see themselves, and the way God sees them. Then I have them write words around the faces to describe each one. It is amazing how many people are harder on themselves than they think others are toward them. Is it because they are putting on a mask so that others will not see their true identity? Or is it because what they think is their true identity is really deception from the enemy? Could it be that they do not show their true selves to others because they perceive a threat of rejection? The key is for them to realize how God truly feels about them. One lady could not even fill out the face representing how God sees her. She said, "I don't even know how God sees me." When we learn what the Bible says about our true identity in Christ, we will be able to release the enemy's lies and receive God's truth about who He created us to be. Likewise, when we embrace the Father's unconditional love for us, we will start loving our true selves and enjoying solitude.

2. I make a conscious effort to be mindful of my self-talk and how it affects me.

You may have heard the old saying, "You are what you eat." I believe this saying is true, but it encompasses more than just the natural food we eat; it also includes the thoughts we continually feast on. Each day the enemy tries to serve us a buffet of assorted thoughts for us to eat, such as those of envy, despair, and anxiety.

We can talk ourselves into or out of anxiety and depression by what we do with toxic thoughts. If we continue to dwell on them and think about all the "what if's" and the "if only's," then our self-talk will affect us adversely. Other examples of negative self-talk include, "Man! I'm such an idiot! I always make a mistake.", or "With my luck, I'll never get a promotion." Sometimes we have a positive thought, but we cancel it out when we add the word "but." For instance, "I got a bonus in my paycheck this month, but it is never enough to pay all my bills!" Instead, the better option is to put the "but" after the negative thought to cancel it out: "I don't know how I am going to pay all my bills, but God is clearly already providing for me with this bonus!" When we filter our self-talk according to Philippians 4:8, we will experience peace and joy.

> *Finally, brothers and sisters, whatever is true, whatever is noble, whatever is right, whatever is pure, whatever is lovely, whatever is admirable—if anything is excellent or praiseworthy—think about such things.*
>
> — *PHILIPPIANS 4:8 (NIV)*

3. I use tools to deal with and minimize stress.

Stress in life can sometimes be positive when it causes us to focus on a task at hand or complete an assignment. However, most stress can be harmful when we do not manage its effects on our physical and mental well-being. Stress chemicals, adrenaline and cortisol, are released in our bodies when we experience stressful situations. They act as an alarm system in our bodies and put us in a survival mode, accompanied by symptoms such as increased heart rate and activated sweat glands. When the perceived danger passes, stress chemical levels drop and our bodies recover. When someone experiences a series of stressful situations, their stress chemicals continue to be released without any reprieve.

This overdose of adrenaline and cortisol increases the risk for multiple health problems, including anxiety, depression, heart disease, cancer, stroke, and more.[7] Stress can actually reduce the size of the brain and impair memory.[8]

Someone who scores a five on this statement is one who knows what triggers stress within her and how to manage it. Some helpful techniques I use with clients include:

- praying
- meditating on God's goodness
- deep breathing (Think of breathing in God's peace and exhaling anxiety.)
- going for a walk in nature
- imagining separating yourself from the stress (Stress is what you deal with, not a part of you.)
- exercising

I love the prescription Paul writes in Philippians for how to handle stress:

> *Be anxious for nothing, but in everything by prayer and supplication, with thanksgiving, let your requests be made known to God; and the peace of God, which surpasses all understanding, will guard your hearts and minds through Christ Jesus.*

> — *PHILIPPIANS 4:6-7*

4. I maintain a healthy diet.

> *Do you not know that your body is the temple of the Holy Spirit who is in you, whom you have from God, and you are*

not your own? For you were bought at a price; therefore glorify
God in your body and in your spirit, which are God's.

— *1 CORINTHIANS 6:19-20*

This statement also includes abstaining from harmful drugs such as nicotine, prescription drugs beyond a doctor's orders, alcohol to the point of drunkenness, and illegal drugs. The verse above says that our bodies are actually the temple of the Holy Spirit. When we harm our bodies by eating an abundance of unhealthy food or taking drugs, we do not honor God, nor do we take care of ourselves.

God made food to nourish our bodies. If we eat a healthy diet, we can actually prevent harmful disease. According to the U.S. Department of Health and Human Services,

> Today, about half of all American adults—117 million people—have one or more preventable, chronic diseases, many of which are related to poor quality eating patterns and physical inactivity. Rates of these chronic, diet-related diseases continue to rise, and they come not only with increased health risks, but also at high cost. In 2008, the medical costs linked to obesity were estimated to be $147 billion. In 2012, the total estimated cost of diagnosed diabetes was $245 billion, including $176 billion in direct medical costs and $69 billion in decreased productivity.[9]

After researching for this chapter, I believe that one of the worst problems with the American diet is the consumption of added sugars. Over-consumption of added sugars in our diet, not counting natural sugar from fruit, leads to diseases such as heart disease, cancer, alzheimer's disease, and aging.[10] The average American consumes 17 teaspoons of added sugar every day (about 71 grams), which totals 57 pounds every year.[11] The American Heart Association suggests we limit our added sugar to 9 teaspoons for males (about 38 grams),[12] 6 teaspoons for females (about 25 grams),[13] 6 teaspoons for children age 2-18,[14] and 0 teaspoons for children under 2.[15]

I am not saying to never consume sugar, but awareness of its effects will help us to be careful of how much we eat and drink. I believe that, for most people, moderation is key. However, if someone is addicted, be it to alcohol, sugar, or any other substance, abstinence is best. I encourage you to check with your doctor for what is best for you.

5. I maintain healthy sleeping patterns.

I will both lie down in peace, and sleep;
For You alone, O Lord, make me dwell in safety.

— PSALM 4:8

It is vain for you to rise up early,
To sit up late,
To eat the bread of sorrows;
For so He gives His beloved sleep.

— PSALM 127:2

Sleep is a gift from God! Just like our technological devices need their batteries recharged daily, our brains need to be recharged as well. In fact, scientists have discovered that as we sleep, the brain is cleansed with a fluid called Cerebrospinal Fluid

(CSF), which takes nutrients to the brain and flushes out waste.[16] Thus, when we have numerous thoughts filling our brain, we can "sleep on it" and have a clearer mind when we wake, in order to make better decisions.

A research study done in the UK showed that "insomnia had a negative effect on people's mood, energy, concentration, personal relationships, ability to stay awake during the day, and ability to carry out daily tasks."[17] We may not realize how our lack of sleep may be harmful to others. Sleep deprivation is often a trigger for frustration and anger that we may direct toward other people.[18] In addition, the National Highway Traffic Safety Administration states that 35,092 people died in car crashes due to drowsy driving in 2015.[19] Hopefully, this knowledge will remind us to prioritize sleep.

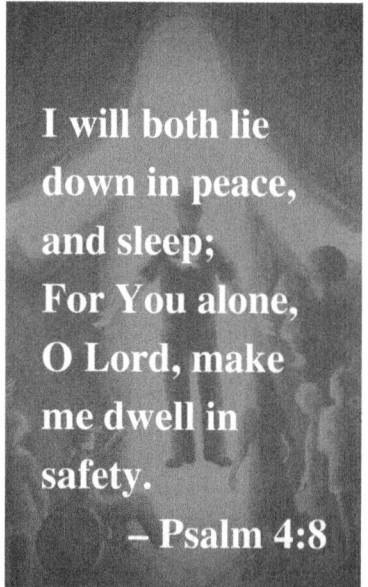

I will both lie down in peace, and sleep;
For You alone, O Lord, make me dwell in safety.

– Psalm 4:8

While it is important to sleep for an average of six to eight hours each night, the Bible also warns us not to sleep too much.[20] Surprisingly, some research shows that people who get more than eight hours of sleep every night also have an increased risk of death.[21] There may be times when we need to sleep longer to help recover from an illness or to catch up on sleep after sleep deprivation. However, sometimes we sleep too long due to lack of motivation. We will soon find that this lack of motivation has robbed us of precious time that could have been invested in building healthy relationships.

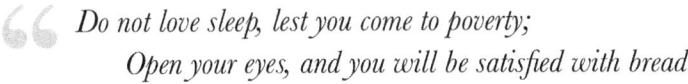

Do not love sleep, lest you come to poverty;
     Open your eyes, and you will be satisfied with bread.

— PROVERBS 20:13

6. I exercise regularly.

Lack of physical activity can produce many harmful conse-quences, hindering our ability to fulfill God's call on our lives. Some people may fear injury if they participate in vigorous, aerobic exercise; however, the risk of chronic illness is far greater than the risk of injury.[22] Of course, it is a good idea to consult a doctor before starting an exercise routine, especially for people with chronic illnesses. Hiring a personal trainer can also help lessen the risk of injury.

In 2018, the Office of Disease Prevention and Health Promo-tion released the second edition of the Physical Activity Guide-lines for Americans. This publication is a free resource that offers a wealth of information about the benefits and guidelines of daily exercise. According to this study, the benefits of at least 150 minutes each week of aerobic activity include:

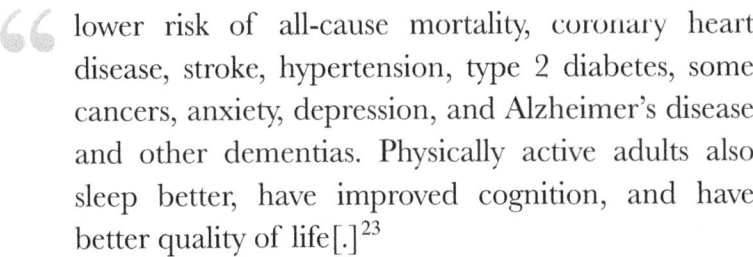

> lower risk of all-cause mortality, coronary heart disease, stroke, hypertension, type 2 diabetes, some cancers, anxiety, depression, and Alzheimer's disease and other dementias. Physically active adults also sleep better, have improved cognition, and have better quality of life[.][23]

How are exercising, eating a balanced diet, and sleeping well related to refining a relationship with self? As we invest in these areas, we demonstrate that we value the gift of life God has given us; thus, if we truly want to refine a relationship with self, we will be motivated to make necessary changes in these areas in order to be a good steward of God's gift of life.

7. I tend to blame myself when I have conflict with others.

When I think of the word "blame," I think of judgement and condemnation. It is not up to us to judge anyone, including ourselves. As mentioned in chapter seven, one unhealthy way to deal with conflict is to blame ourselves for problems in our relationships. Over time, our habit may cause us to take the blame for something we did not do. It is true that we may experience healthy guilt when we need to confess what truly is our fault to God and the other person; however, because God forgives us upon confession,[24] we need to forgive ourselves. Otherwise, we carry unnecessary guilt that keeps us bound. When we are self-critical, we actually hinder God from flowing through us. John explains this beautifully in the following scripture:

> *For if our heart condemns us, God is greater than our heart, and knows all things. Beloved, if our heart does not condemn us, we have confidence toward God. And whatever we ask we receive from Him, because we keep His commandments and do those things that are pleasing in His sight.*
>
> — *1 JOHN 3:20-22*

8. I have inner wounds for which I have not received healing.

Trials happen to all of us periodically throughout our lifespans. Releasing our hurts and offenses allows us to have peace within ourselves and opens the way for us to extend peace to others. The longer we hold on to inner wounds, the longer we will be bound and the harder our journey to healing will be. Think of spilling food on a kitchen counter. If someone wipes the spill immediately, it comes right up without any effort. However, if the food is left on the counter overnight, it may take quite a bit of effort to scrub it off. It the food is left on the counter for days, it may have to be scraped off.

It is common for people to not want to deal with their inner wounds. Over the years of facilitating inner healing with clients, God has uncovered many reasons why they may be holding on to past pains. Some people would rather not face their pain, preferring to repress it and pretend it is nonexistent. Another approach is for the wounded individual to harbor hurts and "nurse" them in order to bring attention to himself and show others that he is a victim. I have seen situations in which when the individual holds on to the pain as a form of "self-protection"; for instance, she may hold on to anger so that others will not get too close and hurt her more. Like a child who will not let her mother remove a splinter for fear that it will hurt, harboring inner wounds is never a wise decision. A person with inner wounds may be uncomfortable facing them and letting them go, but the result is freedom from pain once they are removed and healed.

9. I worry about what others think about me to a degree that interferes with normal, everyday life.

There seems to be an epidemic of people who are bound by what they think other people think of them, partly because they tend to be weighed down by what other people expect from them. This will be covered more in chapter six, but for the purposes of this self-assessment, think about how often you try to live according to the expectations of others. It is easy to get into a rut of thinking we have to please others in order to earn their affirmation and approval. Additionally, some people think they have to prove that they measure up to others. When we care more about what people think than we do what God thinks, we idolize them and serve them instead of God.

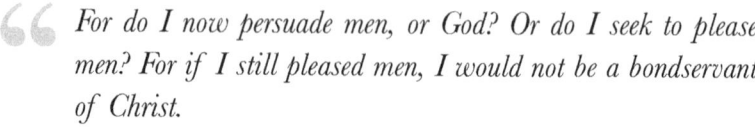

> *For do I now persuade men, or God? Or do I seek to please men? For if I still pleased men, I would not be a bondservant of Christ.*

— *GALATIANS 1:10*

10. I neglect self-care in the area of rest and relaxation.

Our society seems to thrive on being busy. Now, when people are asked how they are doing, more than likely they will say, "Busy!" or "Exhausted!" Studies show that a little over half of American workers do not take all their vacation days.[25] God, Himself, set aside a whole day to rest after He created the Earth and its inhabitants. A day of rest was so important to Him that He included a commandment in the Ten Commandments that tells us to "[r]emember the Sabbath Day to keep it holy."[26] When we do not dedicate time to rest physically, mentally, and emotionally, stress will continue to build up until it has adverse effects on our bodies, minds, and feelings. Additionally, with so many things vying for our attention in all five senses of taste, touch, sight, hearing, and smelling, sometimes we need to take a break from sensory overload, which may include laying down our many technological devices. Finally, when we can be still, take some deep breaths, and allow ourselves to do leisurely activities without any work responsibilities, we will be refreshed to fulfill our obligations later without so much pressure.

11. I feel quite a bit of shame.

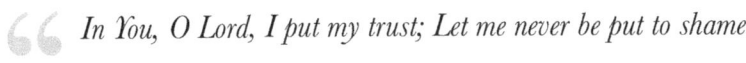 *In You, O Lord, I put my trust; Let me never be put to shame.*

— *Psalm 71:1*

One synonym for "shame" is "humiliation." God wants us to humble ourselves,[27] but He does not want us to humiliate ourselves. Even if other people try to shame us, we can be free of their condemnation when we receive the grace of God. On the back cover of the book, *Free Yourself Be Yourself* by Alan D. Wright is a list of what happens to us when we carry shame:

- Hyper-Sensitivity: Why am I so bothered by every criticism?
- Self-Doubt: Why do I always question my abilities and motives?
- People Pleasing: Why do I have a hard time saying no or facing conflict?
- Fear of Failure: Why do I feel like I have to be perfect?
- Self-Sabotage: Why can't I celebrate my gifts and accept God's blessings?[28]

How can we love ourselves when we feel so shameful? One of the deciding factors in determining when a client is finished with regular therapy sessions is when he is free from shame. This freedom is key in refining a relationship with self.

12. I tend to hold on to anger and either internalize it and be anxious or depressed or take it out on others.

The subject of anger is so important when it comes to relationships that I have devoted chapter nine in this book to address it. Anger in and of itself is not sin. The Bible lets us know that we can be angry and not sin.[29] The problem comes when we hold on to anger and let it have adverse effects on us and on those we love. Just this morning I heard a news report about a lady who ordered a dessert at a fast food restaurant and was infuriated when it took longer to get than she wanted. When she finally received her dessert, she threw it in the server's face and verbally assaulted her. Now, instead of paying just over a dollar for the dessert, she has to pay a fine of over $800 for disorderly conduct.[30] Like this lady, when we act out our feelings of anger, we will find that the price for our explosion exceeds our perceived "reward."

Self-Assessment Statements for Relationship with Self	How often is the statement true? 1 - never 5 - always				
1. I enjoy being by myself.	1	2	3	4	5
2. I make a conscious effort to be mindful of my self-talk and how it affects me.	1	2	3	4	5
3. I use tools to deal with and minimize stress.	1	2	3	4	5
4. I maintain a healthy diet.	1	2	3	4	5
5. I maintain healthy sleeping patterns.	1	2	3	4	5
6. I exercise regularly.	1	2	3	4	5
7. I tend to blame myself when I have conflict with others.	1	2	3	4	5
8. I have inner wounds for which I have not received healing.	1	2	3	4	5
9. I worry about what others think about me to a degree that interferes with normal, everyday life.	1	2	3	4	5
10. I neglect self-care in the area of rest and relaxation.	1	2	3	4	5
11. I feel quite a bit of shame.	1	2	3	4	5
12. I tend to hold on to anger and either internalize it and be anxious or depressed or take it out on others.	1	2	3	4	5

To find your score, take the total scores of statements 1 through 6 and subtract the total scores of statements 7 through 12.

Total score of statements 1-6: _____
Total score of statements 7-12: _____
Final Score: _____

If your score falls between -24 and -8, your ground is ready to be mined for gold! You may not have realized how hard you are on yourself when you neglect self-care and harbor negative thoughts. This new revelation is your first step in allowing God to heal you and prepare you for the fire of refining your relationship with self. Remember that God does not condemn you. He is meeting you where you are and guiding you as you start this journey to inner healing.

If your score falls between -7 and 8, you are in the process of being refined by fire. Impurities have started being removed, but there are still a number of impurities yet to be purged. Seek God's perspective concerning the areas in which your score reflects a need for change. As you go through the fire of refining your relationship with self, remember that the result of refining gold is that the Master Refiner will see His image when He looks at you. This will pave the way to approach your relationships with others in a healthy way.

If your score falls between 9 and 24, you have been through the fire and had many impurities removed. You have already let go of many insecurities that hinder a healthy self esteem. Now God will help you maintain self-care and freedom from offenses. There is always room to grow in the area of loving yourself so that God can flow through you for His glory.

4

REFINING RELATIONSHIPS WITH OTHERS

> Beloved, let us love one another, for love is of God; and everyone who loves is born of God and knows God.
>
> — 1 JOHN 4:7

T HE MAIN OBJECTIVE of this book is to help people develop healthy relationships with others. Because the remainder of this book delineates the principles of functional relationships with others, this chapter will not include as many details as chapters two and three. Like the previous two chapters, I will explain each statement of the self-assessment.

1. I consciously attempt to listen to others without thinking about what I am going to say next.

> So then, my beloved brethren, let every man be swift to hear, slow to speak, slow to wrath.
>
> — JAMES 1:19

It is not difficult to discern when someone you are talking to is not listening as you talk to him; his eyes reveal when he is planning what he is going to say to you instead of listening. I remember that, while teaching elementary school, many of my students would shoot their hands up in the air to answer a question that I was not finished asking! Communication requires talking and listening, and if one person does not listen, the two cannot communicate. Sometimes people are unaware that they do not listen well. Hopefully, rating this statement will draw attention to the issue.

An important aspect of good listening is the ability to understand what you are hearing. Research shows that 90% or more of communication is nonverbal.[1] In order to understand what the speaker is really trying to communicate, we must take into consideration many elements, such as tone of voice, posture, and facial gestures. Even then, we have limited insight into what he is truly feeling. Only God knows all the details of what the person is going through and what is causing him to feel the way he does. I have learned to seek God while someone is talking to me so that I can have better insight into how he feels and thus communicate more clearly. I believe healthy communication is an art and can be developed over time.

2. When in conversation, I consciously try to engage the other person in conversation about himself/herself instead of always talking about myself.

I have to admit that I have not always scored very high on this statement. Ironically, God has called me to a career where my job is to engage the client in conversation about herself and to limit any mention of personal information. Just like people love to hear their names, they also appreciate when you begin conversation by asking about them instead of just telling them about yourself or your family. They especially appreciate when you inquire about something they told you previously. When we only talk about ourselves, we are giving a message, whether we intend to or not, that we do not value the other person. If we truly desire to know the other person, we will listen intently in order to understand her perspective.

3. I am quick to genuinely apologize without adding "but" followed by an excuse.

Ouch! As a marriage therapist, and as a wife, I know that this statement is difficult to attain for most couples. Chapter seven will go into detail about conflict resolution, but for the purpose of understanding this assessment statement, think about how often you apologize to loved ones. I am not talking about constantly blaming yourself because of a low self-image and blurting out, "I'm sorry!" every time you think someone is upset with you; I am talking about apologizing when it is merited. In conflict, both parties are usually at fault to one degree or another. When you realize your fault, simply apologize without conditions. When you say, "I am sorry, but…", you are either adding conditions to your apology, or you are justifying your offense. Adding the word "but" is like cancelling out what comes before it.

You may say, "I'm not going say I am sorry until he does. I am always the one who apologizes first." In that case, if you only apologize when the other person apologizes, your apology is probably not genuine. I frequently tell clients that you cannot change what the other person does or does not do; you can only change yourself.

You cannot change what the other person does. You can only change yourself.

4. I have empathy for people going through difficult times.

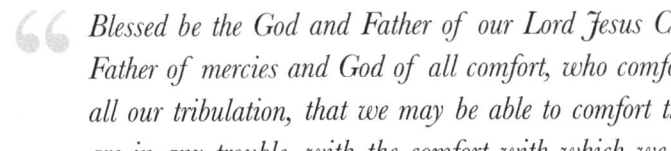

> *Blessed be the God and Father of our Lord Jesus Christ, the Father of mercies and God of all comfort, who comforts us in all our tribulation, that we may be able to comfort those who are in any trouble, with the comfort with which we ourselves are comforted by God.*

— 2 CORINTHIANS 1:3-4

The advantage of enduring the inevitable trials of life is that you can empathize with others who experience similar situations. When you genuinely care about what someone else is going through, you do not have to fix her problem; you simply need to be there for her. Empathizing may mean to intercede in prayer, sit with her in the hospital, or serve her in practical ways. Even if you have experienced a similar situation, you do not have to say that you understand; the only One who truly understands what she is going through is God. He will teach you how to show His love to her. As you allow God to empathize through you, your relationship with her will be blessed.

5. When facing conflict with a friend or family member, I try to give him/her the benefit of the doubt and seek to understand his/her perspective.

Note: If the person with whom you are having conflict habitually lies or manipulates the truth in order to hide something from you, you do not have to be so quick to give him the benefit of the doubt. However, it is a good idea to try to understand his perspective and ask God for wisdom on how to respond.

Conflicts arise for various reasons. As was discussed in

chapter one, conflicts with others often result from differing perspectives. The other person may be experiencing stress from other sources that causes him to be on edge. Another common scenario arises when one person has so many things vying for his attention that he struggles to fulfill the other person's expectations; he inadvertently communicates that he does not value the other person, when, in fact, he does. For instance, a husband tells his wife that he will help her with a household chore. When he receives a phone call, followed by his daughter asking him to help her with a science project, he may legitimately forget about the chore. If he apologizes to the wife and explains the situation, the wife is not giving him the benefit of the doubt if she fires back with comments like: "You always forget! I always have to do the work around here, and you don't even care!" Her comments could easily provoke him to defend his actions, rather than making an effort to prioritize her desires next time. When the wife gives him the benefit of the doubt, she will receive his apology and believe that he did not intentionally neglect helping her. She will then respond with something like, "Thank you for apologizing. It did feel as though you didn't understand my need for help at first, but now that you explained what happened, I feel better about it."

6. I pray for friends and family regularly as the Lord leads.

God is God, and He can do whatever He chooses without our help. However, He chooses to use us through the gift of prayer. I love it when God stirs me to pray a specific prayer and then follows through and answers that prayer in detail. This gift of prayer has helped me tremendously when it comes to refining relationships; when I see prayers for others answered that the Holy Spirit prompted me to pray, my faith grows, and my relationship with God is strengthened. Consequently, my relationships with others are also strengthened.

While writing this portion of the book, I decided to look at what research shows about how often people pray. According to Barna Group, 79% of American adults prayed at least once in three months.[2] Thus, 21% do not pray, and some of the ones who pray only do so once in 3 months! There is no way someone can support his loved ones in prayer if he only prays once a quarter. Barna Group researched all Americans, regardless of religion, but I found a study specifically related to Christians completed by Christianity Today in 2012. The study researched the number of churchgoers that pray for acquaintances who are not Christians:

> 21% of churchgoers say that outside of church worship services they pray every day for people they know who are not professing Christians; 26% say they pray a few times a week; 20% say they rarely or never pray for the spiritual status of others.[3]

While this study does not mention praying specifically for loved ones, any time spent in prayer for others helps to minimize our self-absorption, thus allowing us to develop compassion for them. My prayer is that those who read this book will be stirred to pray more for their loved ones and will receive God's heart for them.

7. I have a hard time being genuinely happy for others when they succeed, especially if I do not share the same success.

> *Who is wise and understanding among you? Let him show by good conduct that his works are done in the meekness of*

wisdom. But if you have bitter envy and self-seeking in your hearts, do not boast and lie against the truth. This wisdom does not descend from above, but is earthly, sensual, demonic.

—*JAMES 3:13-15*

When you truly love someone, you will not envy him.[4] Envy, or coveting other people's possessions or successes, is one of the biggest hindrances to refining relationships. The last commandment of the Ten Commandments tells us not to covet.[5] While the other nine commandments outline actions we should not do, this one concerns the attitude of our hearts. Coveting is an inward disposition that breeds a critical spirit. According to the spiritual law of sowing and reaping,[6] the Bible warns us not to judge others, or we will be judged ourselves.[7] When we realize that all of history is really HIS story, we will then be free to celebrate other people's successes. We will also trust God to unfold our own lives in His timing, and we will be humbled and grateful when He does.

8. I blame the other person in time of conflict.

Just like the old saying goes, "There are always two sides to every story." During conflict between two people, both parties are usually at fault for being selfish to some degree. If nothing else, both parties are probably at fault for not understanding the other person's perspective. Yes, there are times when confrontation is necessary in order to mend broken relationships. However, if we blame the other person when confronting her, she will likely be on the defensive and start blaming us back. We need to first check our own heart motives and determine if we want to tear the other person down or bridge the gap so that we can find a solution together. Instead of attacking the other person's character, we can then lovingly confront her by saying, "I don't know if you meant it this way, but when you said _____, I felt _____." This approach allows the other person to better understand the effect of her actions and respond accordingly. The other person is then free to express how he feels in the relationship as well. By confronting each other healthily, we are building trust that may help lessen the intensity of future conflict.

9. I tend to interrupt others.

For the most part, a person interrupts others in conversation when he does not listen fully; thus, his interjections can be viewed as a sign of not caring what the original speaker thinks or feels. However, the act of interrupting in conversation is perceived differently in people with varying personalities and conversational styles. According to a 2018 research study by  Stanford University doctoral candidate Katherine Hilton, some people approach speaking with high intensity while others are low intensity speakers. Hilton states:

 High intensity speakers are generally uncomfortable with moments of silence in conversation and consider talking at the same time a sign of engagement. Low intensity speakers find simultaneous chatter to be rude and prefer people speak one at a time in conversation.[8]

Those who fall under the category of high intensity speakers need to know that others perceive their interruptions as rude. On the other hand, low intensity speakers need to realize that high intensity speakers do not mean to intrude when they are trying to keep the conversation going. As a person with a high intensity conversational style, I am learning that I need to seek God for what to say, when to speak, and when to stay silent. When I accidentally interrupt, I am learning to simply apologize for the interruption and let the other person continue.

10. I speak before thinking about whether my words will help or hinder my relationships with others.

As was mentioned in chapter three, it is good to filter our self-talk with God's Word. In Matthew 12:34, Jesus said that "out of the abundance of the heart the mouth speaks." Inner healing in our hearts is imperative for our speech to bring forth edification rather than destruction. We can ask ourselves the following questions before speaking to keep us out of trouble in our relationships:

- Is what I am about to say helpful or harmful?
- Am I talking to the right person?
- Am I the right person to say what I am about to say?
- Is this the right time to say what I would like to say?

11. I have unforgiveness toward someone.

The Bible tells us that when we truly love someone, we will not keep a record his wrongs toward us.[9] Holding on to unforgiveness and bitterness ties us to the offender with an unhealthy soul tie. Our soul is made up of our mind, will, and emotions. When we hold a grudge against someone, we are the ones who are bound in our thoughts and emotions; thus, we end up making harmful decisions. On the contrary, when we release and forgive others, we experience incredible freedom!

Two books that have helped me in this area are *Total Forgiveness* by R.T. Kendall[10] and *Forgiving Forward* by Bruce and Toni Hebel.[11] When we do not completely forgive someone, we really have not forgiven them. R.T. Kendall explains how to know if you have totally forgiven someone, and Bruce Hebel uses scripture to show that we will be tormented if we do not forgive. Truly forgiving our offenders will not only free us from living in torment, but it will also position us to have healthy connections with others.

12. I tend to isolate myself and avoid social interaction.

There is always a healthy way and an unhealthy way to look at something. One of the first tactics the devil uses to destroy us and our relationships is to isolate us. However, God loves when we get alone with Him in the "secret place of the Most High."[12] As discussed in chapter nine of this book, Jesus frequently pulled away from the crowds to spend time alone with the Father. If you isolate yourself because you fear what people will think about you, then you need to reframe your time alone and spend that time with God, where you can receive His love, healing, and protection. You may need to seek help from a friend, prayer partner, or professional counselor to help with your journey towards inner healing.

Self-Assessment Statements for Relationship with Others	How often is the statement true? 1 - never 5 - always				
1. I consciously attempt to listen to others without thinking about what I am going to say next.	1	2	3	4	5
2. When in conversation, I consciously try to engage the other person in conversation about himself/herself instead of always talking about myself.	1	2	3	4	5
3. I am quick to genuinely apologize without adding a "but" followed by an excuse.	1	2	3	4	5
4. I have empathy for people going through difficult times.	1	2	3	4	5
5. When facing conflict with a friend or family member, I try to give him/her the benefit of the doubt and seek to understand his/her perspective.	1	2	3	4	5
6. I pray for friends and family regularly as the Lord leads.	1	2	3	4	5
7. I have a hard time being genuinely happy for others when they succeed, especially if I do not share the same success.	1	2	3	4	5
8. I blame the other person in time of conflict.	1	2	3	4	5
9. I tend to interrupt others.	1	2	3	4	5
10. I speak before thinking about whether my words will help or hinder my relationships.	1	2	3	4	5
11. I have unforgiveness toward someone.	1	2	3	4	5
12. I tend to isolate myself and avoid social interaction.	1	2	3	4	5

To find your score, take the total scores of statements 1 through 6 and subtract the total scores of statements 7 through 12.

Total score of statements 1-6: _____
Total score of statements 7-12: _____
Final Score: _____

If your score falls between -24 and -8, your ground is ready to be mined for gold! You have some unhealthy habits that hinder healthy relationships. However, the fact that you picked up this book shows that you are starting the process of developing new habits that will help you relate better to others. You may need to seek professional counseling to help you in your journey towards refinement.

If your score falls between -7 and 8, you are in the process of being refined by fire. Impurities have started being removed, but there are still a number of impurities yet to be purged. This is a good opportunity for you to examine your heart motives. Ask yourself if your motive is to get your own needs met or if you genuinely care about the thoughts and feelings of others. Take some time to thank God for what He has done in your relationships, and ask Him for endurance throughout the refining process.

If your score falls between 9 and 24, you have been through the fire and had many impurities removed. As you continue to seek God for help in areas that may not be completely refined, He will give you the wisdom needed to navigate your relationships. God has placed certain people in your life for a reason. Taking time to maintain healthy relationships with your loved ones is worth every minute.

5

SPIRITUAL WARFARE IN RELATIONSHIPS

> *The thief does not come except to steal, and to kill, and to destroy. I have come that they may have life, and that they may have it more abundantly.*
>
> — *JOHN 10:10*

BEFORE GOD CREATED us, He was a relational being. In Genesis 1:26, God said, "Let Us make man in Our own image." The reference to "us" refers to God the Father, God the Son (the Word), and God the Spirit: the three in one. Since God is relational and we were made in His image, we, too, are relational beings. Genesis 1:27 (NLT) says, "So God created human beings in His own image. In the image of God He created them; male and female He created them." Both male and female carry the image of God. When God created man, He said that it was not good for man to be alone; thus, He created woman from man to be a companion for him. Since relationships are so special to God, it is no wonder that the enemy tries so hard to destroy them.

The things we say and do usually line up with either God's agenda to give abundant life or Satan's agenda to steal, kill and, destroy. I tell my clients to filter their words and actions with this question: "Is what I am about to say/do going to add fuel or water to the fire?" In other words, "Are my words or actions going to tear down or edify?" When our words and actions align with the thief's agenda to steal, kill, and destroy, we are allowing ourselves to be pawns in the enemy's hands, and we can actually grieve the Holy Spirit. When our words and actions line up with God's agenda to give abundant life, we get the privilege of partnering with Him and seeing people set free! Ephesians 4:29-32 spells this out for us:

> *Let no corrupt word proceed out of your mouth, but what is good for necessary edification, that it may impart grace to the hearers. And do not grieve the Holy Spirit of God, by whom you were sealed for the day of redemption. Let all bitterness, wrath, anger, clamor, and evil speaking be put away from you, with all malice. And be kind to one another, tenderhearted, forgiving one another, even as God in Christ forgave you.*

Protection from Spiritual Attack

Psalm 91 is a popular chapter in the Bible depicting protection from spiritual attack. The first two verses describe positioning yourself in a place of safety with God:

> *He who dwells in the secret place of the Most High Shall abide under the shadow of the Almighty. I will say of the LORD, "He is my refuge and my fortress; My God, in Him I will trust."*

The subsequent verses list scenarios from which you will be

protected. Verse five says, "You shall not be afraid of the terror by night, nor of the arrow that flies by day". The Bible uses word pictures to communicate deeper meanings. I believe the word picture in this verse for "the arrow that flies by day" refers to words that people say. One day I was reading Psalm 64 and I found a verse that confirms my conclusion:

Hear my voice, O God, in my meditation;
Preserve my life from fear of the enemy.
Hide me from the secret plots of the wicked,
From the rebellion of the workers of iniquity,
Who sharpen their tongue like a sword,
And bend their bows to shoot their arrows—bitter words,
That they may shoot in secret at the blameless;
Suddenly they shoot at him and do not fear...
But God shall shoot at them with an arrow;
Suddenly they shall be wounded.
So He will make them stumble over their own tongue;
All who see them shall flee away.
All men shall fear,
And shall declare the work of God;
For they shall wisely consider His doing.

— PSALM 64:1-4;7-9 (EMPHASIS ADDED)

There is also a verse from the James 3:8-10 that speaks of how people's words can be destructive:

But no man can tame the tongue. It is an unruly evil, full of deadly poison. With it we bless our God and Father, and with it we curse men, who have been made in the similitude of God. Out of the same mouth proceed blessing and cursing. My brethren, these things ought not to be so.

What a glorious thought to think that people's words do not have to hurt you when you dwell in the secret place of the Most High! Remember who your true enemy is. Your enemy is not the person who said those hurtful words, but it is Satan, who used them for his agenda.[1] God is greater! Satan's word is an arrow, but God's word is a sword that is sharper than any sword you could ever encounter.[2] Has the devil been sending his pitiful arrows to you, telling you that a certain loved one will never change or that your broken connection will never be restored? It is time to answer those arrows with the all-living, all powerful Word of God!

Sometimes we entertain Satan's lies and begin to believe them, essentially making agreement with the lies. When we make agreement with the enemy's taunts, our whole life operates according to that agreement. By listening to the lies and believing them, we are honoring the father of lies[3] rather than the true Lord Jesus Christ. It is important to identify the lies we believe and break agreement with them in Jesus' name. Once those lies are

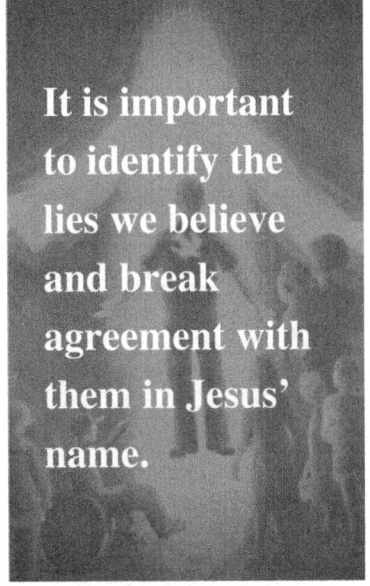

It is important to identify the lies we believe and break agreement with them in Jesus' name.

broken, it is just as important to make agreement with God's truths. If you feel resistance to breaking agreement with lies, there are probably deep wounds which require inner healing. Ask God to reveal the source and origin of each wound and let Him bring His perspective. I encourage you to get a trusted friend, minister, or therapist to help you walk through these steps to healing.

Fear: Satan's Go-To Tool to Destroy Relationships

Faith is God's gift to us that grows from the hope of His unconditional love. On the contrary, Satan wants us to have fear that grows from the despair of isolation; when we allow the enemy to trick us into avoiding others, our fear grows and a destructive cycle begins. Fear of rejection prompts us to isolate ourselves, projecting a message to others to stay away and then causing us to feel rejection and despair. When we find ourselves in this cycle, we tend to focus on rejection more than on God's perfect love; thus, fear overrides faith.

Problems in relationships so often have a root of fear. When I was writing this book, I posted this question on social media: "How does fear affect relationships?". I was surprised with how passionately people responded. Here are just some of many responses:

- Fear makes you afraid to trust because of being hurt, lied to, and betrayed before.
- Fear is a prison. Fear keeps us from moving when we should move or saying what we should say.
- Fear prevents a coming together to resolve a conflict, or to perhaps find out that there never really was a conflict, just a misunderstanding. It isolates the one who is afraid.
- Fear keeps conflict alive.
- Fear freezes. Unable to speak truthfully. Unable to trust. Unable to take action. Always a what if.
- Fear manifests in anger and control.
- Fear can make you numb to reality.
- Each person can bring his/her own fears into the relationship, and their fears collide and cause conflict.

Then the two blame each other for how they feel when it didn't have anything to do with the other person to begin with.

- I used to have a fear of my husband leaving me. I had no signs of anything but devotion from him, but because of my poor self-image, I kept worrying that he would rather have a beautiful, model-type wife instead of me. When I was diagnosed with cancer, my husband (who is never emotional) cried for three days. He held me close, and I comforted him. Through that experience I never again had a fear that he did not love me. Fear was defeated with loyalty, faithfulness, and perseverance!

As I read over these posts, I thought about how fear must be the first weapon the enemy uses to try to destroy relationships. We know it is not God who gives fear because of 2 Timothy 1:7: "For God has not given us a spirit of fear, but of power and of love and of a sound mind." The good news is that as we develop our relationship with God and receive His unconditional love for us, fear cannot stay.

> *There is no fear in love; but perfect love casts out fear, because fear involves torment. But he who fears has not been made perfect in love.*
>
> — *1 John 4:18*

God is the only One who truly loves us with a perfect love. There is nothing we can do to make God love us more than He already does. There is also nothing we can do to make God love us less. When someone really understands this truth and receives

God's love, she realizes there is absolutely nothing to fear. The moment we look to someone else to love us perfectly, fear will start to creep back in, since no human besides Jesus can fulfill our need to be loved perfectly. In other words, the antidote to fear is the perfect love of God; expecting others to love us perfectly will only create more fear.

The Bible has much to say about the dangers of the type of fear that comes from the enemy, but it also has much to say about a positive fear that comes from God (the fear of the Lord). I pondered this and prayed for God's perspective on this paradox. I then had a realization that fear is the act of acknowledging that someone or something has power over you. Think about it: when you fear anything other than God, be it a person, heights, public speaking, spiders, or any situation, you are really believing that whatever you fear is more powerful than you are. However, when you reverently fear the Lord, acknowledging that He has power over your life, you will consequently have peace of mind. Why? First of all, He loves us perfectly—so we know He will never take advantage of us. Secondly, God has ultimate power over all and knows everything; thus, we know that He will protect and guide us into what is best for us.

Here are just a few selections of the Bible's passages about the fear of God:

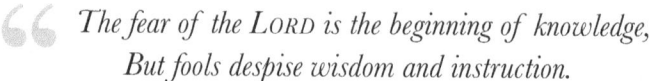

And to man He said,
  "Behold, the fear of the Lord, that is wisdom, and to depart from evil is understanding."

                                                    —Job 28:28

The fear of the Lord is the beginning of knowledge,
  But fools despise wisdom and instruction.

— PROVERBS 1:7

" *In the fear of the LORD there is strong confidence,*
And His children will have a place of refuge.
The fear of the LORD is a fountain of life,
To turn one away from the snares of death.

— PROVERBS 14:26-27

" *Better is a little with the fear of the Lord,*
Than great treasure with trouble.

— PROVERBS 15:16

" *The fear of the LORD leads to life,*
And he who has it will abide in satisfaction;
He will not be visited with evil.

— PROVERBS 19:23

" *Then the churches throughout all Judea, Galilee, and Samaria*
had peace and were edified. And walking in the fear of the
Lord and in the comfort of the Holy Spirit, they were
multiplied.

— ACTS 9:31

When we fear the Lord, we have assurance that He is our refuge and defense. We know this because He is the most powerful being of all. No one is greater. He has the final say over all other gods. When you acknowledge God's power and surrender your life to Him, you can rest assured that you are more than a conqueror through Him![4]

The Importance of Releasing and Forgiving Others

More often than not, you will encounter the issue of unforgiveness in your interactions with other people. Harboring unforgiveness could be an indication that you are not fearing the Lord; when you do not forgive someone, you are giving them power over you rather than fearing God and trusting Him to take care of the offense.

> **When you do not forgive someone, you are giving them power over you rather than trusting God to take care of the offense.**

The Bible reveals that unforgiveness is a device of the devil against us:

> *Now whom you forgive anything, I also forgive. For if indeed I have forgiven anything, I have forgiven that one for your sakes in the presence of Christ, lest Satan should take advantage of us; for we are not ignorant of his devices.*
>
> *— 2 Corinthians 2:10-11*

Every once in awhile, I like to conduct a forgiveness check and ask God to show me if there is anyone I need to forgive. Usually I already know the answer to that question, but sometimes a name will come to mind that I did not think about. The longer I go without forgiving that person, the more bound I am, but as soon as I release and forgive, freedom is mine!

After spending many hours with clients concerning the subject of forgiveness, I have found it helpful for some people to first release the person before actually forgiving him for the wrongs he has done. Releasing a person does not say he is "off the hook," but it says he is "off MY hook." He still has to answer to God for what he did, but it is not my responsibility to make justice happen. I have to trust God and remember that He will execute justice in His timing.

When walking a client through releasing a person, I lead her through a physical action to represent what is happening internally. First, she grasps her hands and holds them close to her chest, as if she is holding on to that person and his wrongs against her. Next, the client prays, preferably out loud so she can actually hear herself say it; I have her open her hands and arms while proclaiming, "I release _____ to You, Lord!" It is amazing to see how this physical action brings such a breakthrough when a client is ready and willing to release the offender. Sometimes the person is hesitant and tells me she cannot do it. In this case, we look for specific hurts connected to the offense. I ask, "What do you think would happen if you did release that person?" Her answer to the question determines which direction to go with inner healing. If you find yourself not being able to release someone who has wronged you, I encourage you to find a professional counselor, coach, or minister who has experience and training in Inner Healing Prayer.

Have I truly forgiven?

Sometimes when I ask a client if he has forgiven a person, he will say, "I thought I did, but I seem to keep having to forgive her, so maybe I haven't." One reason you may feel that you have not forgiven someone is that you still have hurts from what she has done to you. Just because you still feel pain from a relationship does not necessarily mean you have not forgiven the person. Though you may have forgiven your offender, you need to allow deeper inner healing to take place. According to Isaiah 53, Jesus not only bore our sins on the cross, but He also came to bear all our hurts, so why do we keep carrying them?

> *Surely He has borne our griefs*
> *And carried our sorrows;*
> *Yet we esteemed Him stricken,*
> *Smitten by God, and afflicted.*
> *But He was wounded for our transgressions,*
> *He was bruised for our iniquities;*
> *The chastisement for our peace was upon Him,*
> *And by His stripes we are healed.*
>
> — *ISAIAH 53:4-5*

It is time to surrender those hurts to the Lord. One time I had a client that was walking through forgiving her father and releasing hurts. When we took the issue to God in prayer, He revealed a picture of Jesus on the cross, positioned between the two of them and taking her father's beatings on His back. What a breakthrough she had as she realized that Jesus took all the sins from her father, as well as her own hurt, on His back at the cross. She was able to forgive her father *and* let go of all the pain.

Another reason you may have to repeatedly forgive the same person is that, while you may have forgiven him, you may be holding on to the right to not forgive in the future. Imagine you have a container in which you hold your unforgiveness. When you are ready, you pray and ask God to take away all the unforgiveness in the container, and you forgive the offender. However, you still have the container, just in case he offends you again. I encourage you to give the container to the Lord and to choose to forgive once and for all. Finally, ask God to give you a new container from which to hold on to His unconditional love for others.

Inner Healing Prayer

Inner Healing Prayer (IHP) is an intervention that uses a type of listening prayer to receive God's peace-giving perspective. One client said that Inner Healing Prayer was "the single most life-changing awareness process" of her life. While there may be a facilitator helping to lead prayer, the Holy Spirit is the true counselor; thus, lay people, ministers, and life coaches can be trained in IHP. Individuals can also learn to use IHP for themselves without a facilitator. I use Inner Healing Prayer frequently for myself by asking God what He wants to say or show me about why I feel a certain way when facing a difficult or confusing situation. Note: It is not my intention to use this book to train people in Inner Healing; I offer weekend training seminars for this purpose.

People often ask me if Inner Healing Prayer is the same thing as deliverance ministry. It depends on your definition of deliverance. Most people I have encountered with deliverance ministry focus on demonic activity and praying against demons (fallen angels) in a person's life. In my experience, inner healing is more about breaking agreement with lies the person is believing and making agreement with truth. When the person makes agreement with truth, demons do not have any grounds to stay because the only power they have is deception. Remember what Jesus said, "You shall know the truth, and the truth will set you free!" [5]

If demons are cast out, but the root of why they were there to begin with is not dealt with, then they will return. It is like a pile of trash that has flies swarming around and rodents rummaging through. You can go out and shoo the flies and rodents away, but if you do not take away the trash, they shall return! We must remember that Jesus crushed the head (authority) of the enemy on the cross. He took the keys to death, hell, and the grave. His power is greater than any demon that comes your way. Yes, demons will continue to come against us, but our focus needs to be on the Deliverer more than on the schemes of the enemy.

After inner healing, if there still seems to be demonic activity lingering around, then make a declaration like: "I break agreement with the spirit of fear [or whatever it is coming against you]! Fear is no longer part of my identity and has no authority in my life. I receive the unconditional love of God that casts away all fear. Because of the shed blood of the Lord Jesus Christ, fear has to leave, in Jesus's Name!" At this point in a session, I usually have the client open his hands in a receptive mode, and I pray, "Lord, he just let go of fear [or whatever it was] that he has been holding on to for a long time. What do You have in place of what he just released?" The person usually senses what it is that God has for him and tells me. I then ask if he can receive it, and I have him thank God for the exchange. He has then been delivered, not by focusing on demonic activity, but by inviting the Holy Spirit to reveal truth.

Prayer

Almighty God, thank You for creating us in Your image as relational beings. I know that relationships are of utmost importance to You, and so does the enemy. I come against the enemy's agenda to steal, kill, and destroy, and I make agreement with the abundant life You offer me. I do not want the fear the enemy wants to give me. I want to have a holy fear of You and You alone. I declare that no one, no thing, and no circumstance has any power over me outside of You. I accept your perfect love and surrender my life afresh and anew to You, trusting You to protect and guide me. Open my spiritual eyes to see what is truly going on, and open my spiritual ears to hear Your divine direction as I interact with others. Help me to release and forgive others as You prompt me to do so. I look to You to love others through me as I receive Your love in the name of Jesus, Amen!

6

HIDDEN EXPECTATIONS

> *...being confident of this very thing, that He who has begun a good work in you will complete it until the day of Jesus Christ.*

> — *PHILIPPIANS 1:6*

W E NEED TO remember that God is the One who does transforming work within us. Not only does He start the transformation, but God has also promised to complete the work He starts. Our progress does not depend on what others do. In the midst of a dysfunctional relationship, it is easy to fall into the trap of believing that we cannot heal from inner wounds or make any forward progress until the other person changes. Essentially, we are then looking to people for our hope instead of Jesus, the author and perfecter of our faith.[1]

When we dwell on other people's need for change, we may not even realize that we are placing expectations on them in our subconscious mind. When those hidden expectations are not met, disappointment arises, breeding dissatisfaction and possibly despair. As long as we are unaware of the expectations we have placed on others, we will also be unaware that we may be the ones who are hindering progress by looking to people instead of God. This confusion prevents true communication from occurring and perpetuates an unhealthy cycle of blaming others, which counselors refer to as blame-shifting.

Progress happens when we seek God for His perspective of what is truly happening. When God shows us the expectations we have placed on others and why, it is then our responsibility to surrender them to God and trust Him to give us wisdom. If we do not release the revealed expectations to God, then we have an issue with control. People who are not Christians may not see anything wrong with the desire to control one's own life. However, as believers

The more we release control over to God, the more freedom we experience.

we learn that the more we release control over to God, the more freedom we experience. As we surrender control, we will also grow in our ability to surrender unhealthy thoughts and expectations.

The Role of Thoughts in Relationships

In Cognitive Behavioral Therapy (CBT), therapists are trained to help clients become aware of how their thoughts affect their emotions and behaviors. When processing thoughts with clients according to CBT, we look at patterns of problematic thinking that can breed negative emotions. Common patterns include:

- Jumping to Conclusions - You predict what is going to happen before the conclusion.
- Mind reading - Someone says or does something, and you think you know what they are thinking and feeling.
- All or nothing - If everything you want to happen occurs, you are happy; if one negative thing happens, you are upset.
- Exaggerating - You give negative experiences more attention and blow them out of proportion.
- Minimizing - You give positive experiences less attention and discount steps of progress.

Most people do not realize they have such detrimental patterns of thinking. They also may not realize that their negative thinking is just as much the cause of dysfunction in the relationship as the other person's faults. I encourage you to ask God to reveal your tendencies toward these patterns and how they may be influencing your relationships.

I often see how problematic thinking patterns affect relationships, especially in marriages. For example, if Susie operates in an "all or nothing" mindset, she will be quick to say to her husband things like, "You always forget to take out the trash!" or "You never listen to me!" Carrying this example further, Susie can follow suit with the pattern of "mind reading" and think, "My husband does not care about me. He does not think what I have to say is important." The more Susie dwells on these negative thoughts, the more she nags her husband to change his ways. Then, before she realizes it, she ends up complaining about her husband to other people who do not know what to say to her. What began as mere thoughts end up tearing down the foundation of Susie's marriage.

When we allow these thought patterns to influence a relationship, our tendency is to be critical of the other person; thus, we build up more negative expectations that can easily send a message of despair. I challenge clients to be intentional about changing the way they think about specific relationships and to look for and acknowledge the good in other people.

Releasing Expectations in Order to Release and Forgive Others

As mentioned in the chapter on spiritual warfare, it is important to release and forgive other people. Sometimes it is difficult to release people because they do not meet our expectations. In that case, we need to first release our expectations of them before we can forgive. Suppose a husband has certain expectations for what he wants or needs in a wife. Even if his wife meets most of those expectations, no wife could meet all of them because no human is perfect. As illustrated in Figure 6-1 below, whether she meets 90% of his expectations or just 30%, the difference between his desires and what she actually meets leaves an emptiness that leads to disappointment.

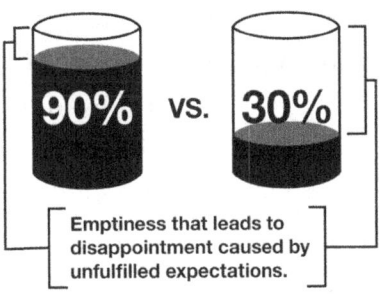

Figure 6-1

What this husband may not realize is that if each partner in a marriage looks to God to meet his/her needs and stops expecting the other to complete him/her, then two whole people come together to make an incredible union. This is especially true in marriage, but it pertains to any relationship. Though difficult, I encourage you to release all the expectations you have placed on people over to God and trust *Him* to meet your needs. Though God sometimes uses people to meet your needs, He can also meet your needs without people. Either way, you can remember that God is your source for satisfaction!

Sometimes, after several of our expectations are not met, we start expecting a loved one to *not* meet them. In other words, we have two sets of expectations: our original expectations on the person and our expectation that they will fail to fulfill them. We are then in bondage because of the conflict between our two sets of expectations. The enemy convinces us through negative self-talk that they will fail us, with such thoughts as:

- "My daughter will never listen to me."
- "My husband does not value me."
- "My supervisor will not even notice what I do."

Consequently, we speak these lies directly to the people who upset us and to others about them. They begin to identify with our accusations and even fulfill them. What if, instead of accusing our loved ones, we speak truths from the Word of God over them? Even if we do not see them exhibiting the truths we proclaim, our obedience to align with God's thoughts about our loved ones can help to transform both parties' attitudes and remind us that change is possible.

When I explain the importance of releasing expectations, I sometimes have a client who struggles to grasp the concept. For example, a parent may say, "Isn't my job to teach my child to fulfill certain expectations? After all, I am there to help prepare him for life. One day a boss will have expectations over him." While it is true that as parents we need to teach our sons and daughters certain standards, the problem arises when we take responsibility to control our kids. We need to examine our motives. Do we want them to be prepared for life, or do we want them to "act right" for the sake of our own reputation, believing that our children's behavior is a reflection on us as parents? God will show us our heart motives if we seek Him.[2] He will give us the grace we need to release control and expectations of our children over to Him.

Imagine opening your hands in front of you with your palms up. You hold the set of expectations you may teach your children in your hands. Your hands are not grasping those expectations but merely allowing them to be there. Now, say a prayer asking God to reveal to you His standards for your children and any extra expectations you have placed on them that are not from Him. While it is your responsibility to teach your child in the ways of the Lord, it is not  your responsibility to make sure he is successful in life. Your child has a free will of his own. When he chooses something you would not prefer, his actions provide opportunities for you to demonstrate your unconditional love by releasing and forgiving him. Keep surrendering him to the Lord and watch what the Lord can do!

The act of releasing both the person and your expectations allows an avenue for true forgiveness, whether the offender has apologized or not. The offender may have neglected to do for you what he should have done (omission), or he may have committed actions against you that he should not have done (commission). Ask God to reveal to you all the wrongs the person has done against you, whether through omission or commission, and say a prayer to God forgiving him. Include in the prayer that the person is no longer in debt to you, and pray a blessing over him.

NOTE: For more instructions on forgiveness, I recommend following the "7 Protocols of Forgiveness" found in Bruce and Toni Hebel's book, *Forgiving Forward: Unleashing the Forgiveness Revolution*.[3]

Expectations Placed on Us

While the enemy uses the expectations we place on people to keep them bound, he also uses expectations placed on us to keep us bound. I remember one lady I counseled who was weighed down by all the expectations her mother placed on her. She shared a memory of a time when her mom inspected all the dishes she washed and got upset with her because there was a spot on one of the plates. The mother made the daughter remove every dish from the cupboards and wash them all again by hand. The daughter carried a message for years that she was not good enough and would never measure up. Finally, after an extended journey of healing, the daughter has released all of the expectations placed on her by her mother and is even in ministry, helping others in their journey to freedom!

You may not be able to relate to the story above, but everyone has had expectations placed on them. You may even feel crushed by others' standards because you cannot live up to them. Sometimes you need to crawl out from under the expectations others have placed on you to be the "perfect" spouse, parent, friend, or employee. Yes, God does want to use you in those roles, but remember that He is the source of their fulfillment through you.

When you cannot be the husband/wife your spouse needs or the parent your child needs, God can make up for your inabilities and fulfill their needs nonetheless. You can trust God to take care of your loved ones, both through you and without you, when you surrender what others expect you to do over to Him. Tremendous freedom awaits you when you no longer have others' expectations weighing you down!

Expectations Placed on Self and Impending Inner Vows

Sometimes the expectations burdening us are self-inflicted. If we do not release other people's expectations over us, we tend to agree with them and even add more. Their expectations then become our own. When we do not reach these standards, we may have a hard time forgiving ourselves. I often have clients who struggle frequently with guilt and shame from past mistakes, whether real or perceived. Even if they believe that God has forgiven them, they still do not forgive themselves.

When we place expectations on ourselves, we often unknowingly make unhealthy vows. God takes vows very seriously. Inner vows that do not align with His truth will rob us of the freedom Christ died to give us. We must renounce such vows as soon as we discover them and recommit to God's truth. One lady told me how God revealed an undetected vow she made as a young girl during a time of her parents' marital dysfunction. One day when she was sick, she noticed that both of her parents showed concern for her and stopped fighting with each other, so she made an inner vow that she would always be sick in order for her parents to stop arguing. After that vow, she carried many health problems into her twenties and had more prescriptions for illnesses than some senior citizens. After she realized that she made a vow as a young girl, she renounced the vow and broke agreement with it. God actually healed her inner wounds *and* her physical illnesses. She was so excited to tell me how many prescription drugs she did not have to take anymore!

Another example of an inner vow was revealed during an Inner Healing Prayer session I facilitated with a lady whose brother died tragically years earlier. The Lord took her to a memory of a vow she made that she would never love with her whole heart again because she did not ever want to hurt like she did after her brother's death. Two years later, she delivered her first baby. God showed her how the vow she made caused her to have a fear of loving her daughter because she worried that if her baby died of SIDS (Sudden Infant Death Syndrome), she would not be able to bear the pain. This vow continued to affect relationships with people who loved her dearly, until she followed the protocol to break the vow: she confessed her vow, asked God to forgive her, renounced the vow, broke agreement with the fear, and made agreement with God's perfect love and protection. (A prayer for breaking vows is included at the end of this chapter.)

While inner vows often affect us negatively, healthy vows can have a positive affect. For example, one person vowed after a divorce to never allow Jesus to take a back seat to anything ever again. She had married someone she met in Bible college. Though they were involved in all areas of Church ministry, they did not keep Christ at the center of their marriage and eventually divorced. She is now happily married to someone who agrees with her vow, and they continue to let God be the Lord of their marriage.

Fulfilling Our Roles

As was previously mentioned, God wants to use us in specific roles, whether as a son/daughter, spouse, parent, or friend. In these roles, we can either operate from a self-focused motive, acting according to our own agenda, or a God-focused motive, seeking Him for what we should say or do. We need to surrender our agenda to God, trusting Him to take care of our needs. Without surrendering to God's purpose for us within a specific relationship, we will not be fully satisfied in that role and can easily fall into the trap of blaming the other person in the relationship. We can surrender to God through prayer and by seeking Him for what to say and do. When we do, we allow His true unconditional love, to both satisfy us within the role and help us to truly love others, flaws and all!

We must each ask ourselves, "How much am I allowing God to direct me in how I am supposed to fulfill this role, and how much am I deciding for myself what to do?" You may be thinking, "Well, I have been praying for my relationship for years, and God is not doing anything about it!" In that case, it is time to step back and examine the heart motive in your prayers. If you are praying from a self-focused motive rather than a God-focused motive, your prayers are in vain. For example, if you are praying for your spouse to change, ask yourself, "Am I praying so that it will be easier on me, or am I praying for him to change because I love him and want him to be free?" God is not obligated to answer prayers that do not originate from the Holy Spirit; we have to pray according to His will.[4] Maybe this is what John the Baptist meant when he spoke of Jesus and said, "He must increase, but I must decrease."[5]

I encourage you to take some time now to think about how much you surrender control to God within a difficult relationship. On a scale of 0-10, with 0 representing you trying to personally control the relationship and 10 representing full surrender to God, where do you rate yourself? Be truthful! This exercise can be eye-opening. Even so, as we examine our heart motives, it is important to give ourselves grace and remember that releasing control is a process. As we continue surrendering to God, we will experience freedom as we release unrealistic expectations of self and others.

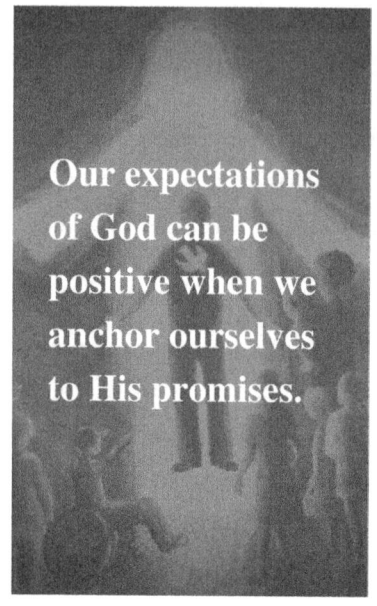

Our expectations of God can be positive when we anchor ourselves to His promises.

Expectations Placed on God

Some people have a hard time giving control over to God because, whether they realize it or not, they have expectations on God that need to be addressed first. Our expectations on God can affect our relationship with Him negatively or positively. If we use our prayer time to tell God how we want Him to fix our problems, we may be disillusioned in our walk with Him when He does not answer our prayers according to our expectations. I have seen people actually turn away from God when He did not answer their prayers according to their preferred method or timing. They forget about the fact that God sees the bigger picture and may, in fact, be protecting them; thus, they tend to blame God when things do not go their way.

On the contrary, our expectations of God can be positive when we anchor ourselves to His promises. For example, we know that He will never leave us or forsake us,[6] so we can expect Him to be with us no matter what trials come our way. We also know that He will use whatever happens to us, whether good, bad, or indifferent, for our good and His glory.[7] Of course, during a trial, tumultuous events may veil the reality of God's presence with us, but in these moments we must be led by His truths instead of our hijacked mind and emotions. I have witnessed many Inner Healing Prayer sessions where God takes a person back to a traumatic memory and simply lets her know that He was there with her, even though she did not realize it. The person experiences freedom as she exchanges the despair from her time of trauma for God's perfect peace. She now realizes that He is always with her and will see her through difficult situations.

Prayer for releasing expectations:

Dear Lord, forgive me for placing expectations on _____ for what I want him/her to be as a _____ (spouse, parent, child, friend). I release those expectations to You and trust You to meet my _____ (husband/wife, mother/father, son/daughter, friend) needs. While I know that You want to use _____ in the role of _____ , I also know that when _____ does not have what it takes to meet my needs, You make up for his/her lack. When You do use _____ to meet my needs, it is a bonus, and I will remember that You are ultimately the source of the love shown to me through him/her. In Jesus' Name, Amen!

Prayer for releasing expectations placed on self by others:

Dear Lord, thank You for showing me how I have been burdened under the expectations placed on me to be a good _____ (spouse, daughter/son, parent, friend). While I know that You want to use me in that role, I also know that I *will* fall short and let _____ (my spouse, parent, child, friend) down. Please remind me that when I do what You prompt me to say or do for _____ I am allowing You to love him/her through me. Thank You for making up for my lack when I do not have what it takes to meet his/her needs. I release any control or responsibility on my part that You never intended for me to carry, and I trust

You to work in our relationship according to Your will. In Jesus' Name, Amen!

Prayer for renouncing unhealthy vows:

Dear Lord, thank You for revealing to me the unhealthy vow I made of _____ . I confess this vow and ask You to forgive me for believing the lie that says _____. I renounce the vow and break agreement with _____ (any lie or negative emotions resulting from the vow). I make agreement with Your truth that says, _____. In Jesus' Name, Amen!

Prayer of thanksgiving:

Heavenly Father, thank You for sending Your Son, Jesus Christ, to give His life so that we can have abundant life! Thank You for also sending Your Holy Spirit to dwell within us and point us to Christ. Because of the blood shed by the Lord Jesus Christ, I can break agreement with the lies of the enemy and be free from the bondages of unhealthy expectations and vows. Please make me hungry and thirsty for more of You in my life as I continue to look for guidance in Your Word, prayer, and worship over time. Thank You that in Your presence is fullness of joy! In Jesus' Name, Amen!

7

DEALING WITH CONFLICT

> *Behold, how good and how pleasant it is*
> *For brethren to dwell together in unity!*
>
> — *PSALM 133:1*

OVER SEVEN BILLION people live in this world, and yet no two people are exactly alike—not even "identical" twins. Some people are spontaneous, while others are more structured. Some people are loud and boisterous, while others are quiet and reserved. Some people are risk-takers, while others are extremely cautious. The list goes on and on. Such diverse personalities provide opportunities for conflict to occur between people. Like the contrasting colors in a beautiful tapestry, conflict can actually be positive if we celebrate our differences instead of judging those different from us.

We need unity, not uniformity. Whereas uniformity implies that everyone is the same, unity implies that different people are working together harmoniously. In Psalm 133, the psalmist says that unity leads to "life forevermore!"[1] We can impact the world dynamically when we bring our differences together in unity. Just like tension in a bowstring causes an arrow to be shot with more power and precision, the tension between two different people will increase their influence. Whether their influence will be positive or negative depends on whether they respect each other's differences or oppose each other in disagreement.

Problematically, every one of us has a natural tendency to pridefully consider our way as the best way.[2] However, God has taught me that He utilizes the very mannerisms that irritate me in other people for good. When I observe God using these mannerisms, I will stop being so critical and actually start appreciating them. I have also started becoming more aware of how my own mannerisms may irritate someone else from a different persuasion. Thus, I try to be intentional in humbly living the way God created me, instead of operating with a haughty attitude that my way is the "right" way. I can then live with purpose, knowing that I fulfill a role that no one else can fulfill because of how God uniquely created me.

God uses each of us in our differences to form a team that will bring more people. For example, one person we will call "Meticulous Mindy" thinks that she is late to an event if she is not ten minutes early, while another person we will call "Spontaneous Sue" usually runs out the door ten minutes before an event. Mindy may be critical of Sue, but Sue's spontaneous disposition can be advantageous. If a Sunday School teacher cannot make it to church at the last minute, "Spontaneous Sue" would be the one to fill in. "Meticulous Mindy" would not consider teaching the class unless she had one month's notice; however, she can help by greeting the children when they arrive and by giving them a coloring sheet until Sue gets there. When Mindy and Sue appreciate each other's strengths and work together instead of criticizing each other, they can accomplish great things.

What to Do About Confrontation

Conflict is bound to happen between two people; thus, confrontation is sometimes necessary. Confrontation usually has a negative connotation, but we can consider certain things that will help to make confrontation a positive experience. In a recent marriage counseling session, the wife was upset because the husband did not communicate with her. The husband said, "I HATE confrontation with a passion!" I said to him, "What if, instead of the two of you confronting through accusation and yelling, you could communicate with each other in a such a way that brings insight and lessens misunderstandings?" His eyes lit up and he exclaimed, "I would love that!" After teaching the principles of this chapter, I mediated a confrontation between them that resulted in mutual understanding.

Before we confront anyone, we need to check our heart motives. I have learned to ask myself, "Am I just thinking about my own needs, or do I genuinely care as much for the other person as I care about myself?" When I am as concerned about hearing and understanding the other person as I am about being heard, I can proceed with confrontation. Genuine communication calls for mutual respect.

When I confront someone without respecting him, my confrontation can become aggressive and reveal an attitude that only my needs and desires matter. I will become haughty and unapproachable, and I may revert to using control and manipulation. On the other hand, if I approach conflict passively, I will not confront the other person at all. Thinking that the other person's needs matter more than mine, I will defer to him when confronted and will become a "doormat" for him to walk on. The healthier option is to respect the other person *and* myself by approaching confrontation assertively. Assertiveness training teaches me that, though the other person's needs and desires are important, my needs and desires are equally important. If both people mutually respect each other, confrontation will be a healthy tool for successful communication, further refining the relationship.

When I truly care about understanding the other person, I will desire to validate her emotions. Everyone needs validation. However, validation does not mean I have to agree with the other person; it merely means I let her know that I understand why she thinks or acts the way she does. Validation will help motivate the other person to want to work the conflict out between us. On the contrary, accusation can offend the other person and hinder his desire to find middle ground.

When we validate the other people, we show that we value them. Sometimes what we say we value and what our actions prove we value are two different things. Here are some examples of the conflict between what we say we value and what our actions show:

- Someone may say he values good health, but he does not make time for regular exercise, nor does he avoid foods that he knows are harmful to his body.
- Someone may say she is a Christian and that she values her faith, yet she goes days without spending time with God in prayer and Bible study. She also rarely shares her faith in Christ with others.
- Someone may say he values time with family, but he works so hard that he stays at the office past closing time, and he brings more work home. Even when he is in the house with his family, he is still sometimes an absent father.

Especially in regards to relationships, we need to examine our values. Ask yourself, "Do I value this relationship or being right more?" One husband admitted that before learning these princi-ples, his objective was to win the fight when he and his wife were discussing issues in their marriage. Now his objective is to better understand and validate his wife.

To communicate healthily, we need to filter everything that comes in our ears and guard everything that comes out of our mouths.[3] This is where prayer comes in. We need to seek God to give us understanding about what we hear and to guide us in what we say. Sometimes He will let us know what *not* to say and how to pray instead. We will be better off in our relationships if we speak more heartfelt compliments to the other person and release our complaints to God. Our challenge is to avoid taking the other person's comments personally. We also do not need to speak words with the intent of offending the other person. We may not admit to the latter, but when we say anything in a critical spirit, we project a message that we want to provoke the other person, treating him as an enemy. Remember who the true enemy is! It is not the other person who misunderstands you; it is the devil and his demonic troops that want to steal, kill, and destroy your relationships.

Where is Your Focus During Conflict?

There are three basic ways we can handle conflict with another person, two of which are unhealthy and one that is healthy. Each scenario describes our focus during conflict. The following sections explain each approach and their consequences:

1. Focus on the Other Person as the Problem: Judging the Other

The first model, as depicted in Figure 7-1, occurs when we focus on the other person as being the problem. This act of constantly blaming the other person prevents us from seeing any weaknesses in ourselves and fosters a critical spirit, producing unforgiveness, bitterness, and anger. These emotions result in anxiety, which either leads to giving the other person "the silent treatment" or coming against him with aggression. The worst-case scenario ends in murder. Even if we would never think of killing someone in conflict, we may not realize that when we constantly blame someone, we suffer from the same seed of resentment as a murderer. We may not kill the person, but we are definitely killing the relationship.

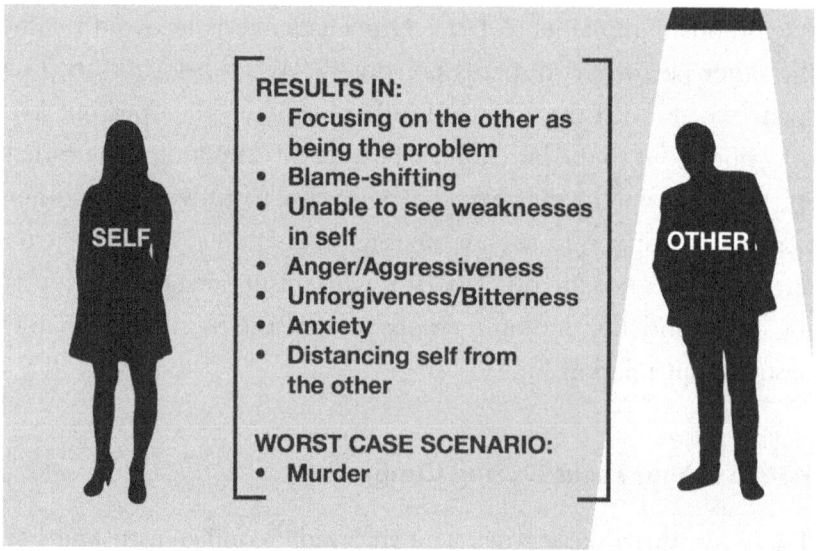

Figure 7-1

2. Focus on Self as Being the Problem: Judging Self

Figure 7-2 illustrates the second model of handling conflict, which is when we put the spotlight on ourselves as being the problem. This is when we keep saying, "If only I had..." We take the blame and become a doormat in the relationship. Self-condemnation, shame, and the constant feeling of not being good enough can lead to a depression that results in harboring a "victim mentality." Our tendency, then, is to isolate ourselves not just from the other person, but from anyone. The worst case scenario ends in suicide. Even if we do not commit suicide, we are planting the same seed of condemnation in ourselves when we constantly judge ourselves as being the problem. Self-condemnation also destroys the relationship with the other person.

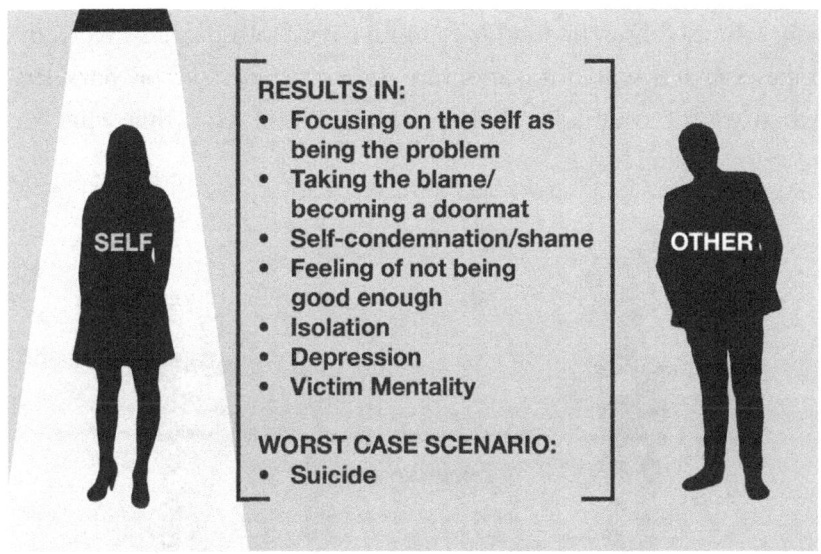

Figure 7-2

3. Focus on God to Reveal and Heal: Let God be the Judge

> *Therefore judge nothing before the time, until the Lord comes, who will both bring to light the hidden things of darkness and reveal the counsels of the hearts. Then each one's praise will come from God.*
>
> — *1 Corinthians 4:5*

It is time to let God handle conflict His way! In the third model, we focus on God instead of judging the other person or ourselves as being the problem (see Figure 7-3). As we focus on God and His perspective, He will shine His light on the problem *and* on the solution! We will better understand the underlying problems of our conflict and receive the wisdom to know how to handle them. As 1 Corinthians 4:5 says, not only will God show us the bigger picture about the issue, but, without condemnation, He will also show us the heart motives of both parties involved.[4] Likewise, we will not condemn the other person or ourselves when we see what is really happening. Thank God that what He reveals, He heals!

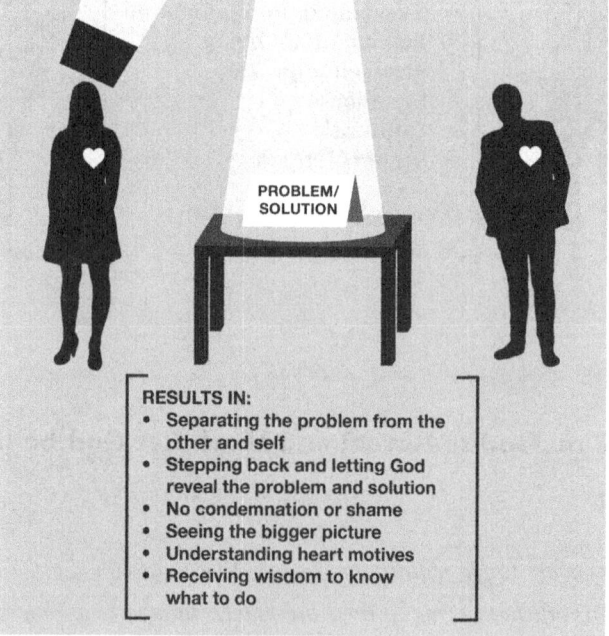

Figure 7-3

If you are in a situation in which the other person is not willing to make an effort to improve the relationship, you can still use this third model of dealing with conflict. When you focus on God and let Him provide insight on how to handle the situation, you are better equipped to release control, as discussed in chapter six. Obviously, if both parties follow these principles, the relationship will improve more and in less time than if only one person follows suit. However, never underestimate what God can do through one person whose heart is committed to follow His lead!

Reflective Listening

In order for communication to be successful, information has to be presented, received, and understood. I am writing this book as a way of communicating to the readers how to refine their relationships. This information will do no good until someone reads it, comprehends it, and applies it to his life. Likewise, if someone presents information through speaking, she will only be communicating if someone else listens to her and understands what she is saying. We have classes in school to teach us how to write, read, and speak, but how often do schools offer a class on listening? Everyone wants to be heard. The problem is, not very many people listen well. The Bible tells us the importance of listening in the book of James, where we are told to be quick to hear and slow to speak.[5] When we speak before we listen, we can provoke anger that negatively affects relationships.

I do not recall receiving any training on effective listening before pursuing a counseling degree. I then learned about a technique called "Reflective Listening" as a way to develop empathy for the client. In reflective listening, the listener's job is to listen to the speaker in order to understand his perspective and feelings. Before responding, the listener reports back to the speaker what she heard and asks the speaker if what she heard was correct. If it was not correct, the speaker clarifies what he said, and the listener again reflects back what she heard him say. The listener can then proceed to reflect back what she sensed the speaker was feeling for further clarification. After practicing reflective listening in the counseling setting, I began to think about how valuable this technique could be for everyday life.

There is nothing more frustrating than when you talk to someone and see in his eyes that he is not listening. Sometimes you can tell that instead of listening he is formulating a rebuttal of what he wants to say back to you. Other times, the person you are trying to talk to interrupts you with his own conversation, proving he was not listening to you. Even as I write this, I realize that I have been guilty of not listening well to others. I know I *can* listen attentively, because when I am in a counseling session with a client I am operating in the best listening skills so that I do not harm the client. What is the difference? When I am in a session with a client, I think, "I am here for you." However, when I am not in a counseling session, sometimes I focus solely on my own thoughts and feelings in a situation, rather than focusing on what the other person is saying and feeling.

When using the reflective listening technique, one person "gets the floor" to communicate his perspective. The other person listens intently to the speaker and then reflects back what he heard. When the listener understands what the speaker said and felt, she responds to that message. The speaker and listener can then swap positions in order for the listener to also be understood.

Guidelines for Reflective Listening

For the Speaker:

- Pray and ask God if this is the right time to approach the other person. If so, ask the other person in a non-threatening way if he has time to talk or when a better time would be.

- If this is about a conflict within the relationship with the listener, choose one issue to address. Too often people address multiple issues at one time, making it difficult for the listener to know which issue to answer.
- Pray and ask God to give you the words to say and the manner in which to say them.
- Start with a disclaimer like, "I may be wrong, but from my perspective…" or "I'm not sure you meant it this way, but…"
- Refrain from accusing the other person (or another person you are talking about). For example, instead of saying, "You don't care!," say, "I know you care about me, but when you said _____, it made me feel like you did not care about me."

For the Listener:

- Pray and ask God to give you ears to hear what the speaker is saying.
- Pray and ask God to help you not to take this personally.
- Refrain from becoming defensive or planning a rebuttal. Avoid giving nonverbal cues that show disrespect for the speaker, such as rolling your eyes, shaking your head, or raising your voice.
- Reflect back to the speaker what you heard by saying, "What I heard you say was _____. Is that correct?"
- Reflect back to the speaker what you think he feels.
- Respond to the speaker. This is when you validate what the speaker feels, even if you do not agree. If

what the speaker said was about you, you may apologize if necessary. Your apology needs to be heartfelt and without excuses; saying, "I am sorry, but…." cancels out the apology. If you do not feel you did anything that demands an apology, you can say, "I am sorry you felt that way." Do not counter-attack during this time by telling the speaker where she is in the wrong.

The guidelines listed are helpful when you have a conflict with someone and you want to establish mutual understanding with him. However, there are situations where it is best if you do not confront the person. For instance, someone with a personality disorder or unhealed inner wounds is not in a position to listen objectively to what you have to say. Many times, a person in this position does not think he needs help; rather, he may think everyone else is to blame. Instead of confronting, take time to seek God alone, surrendering your burdens and asking Him to help you love the other person as He loves her.

Another scenario when it is best not to confront a person is when the person is merely being herself and has no ill-will against you at all. In this case, you may cause harm if you bring your offense to his attention. Pray and ask God if you should approach him or not. The Holy Spirit will either give you a release in your spirit to confront, or He will put a check in your spirit not to confront. Your offense may be stemming more from your own inner wounds than from the actions of the other person. God wants to bring you truth that will set you free from the lies of the enemy. You can always seek professional counseling to help you walk through these situations and bring clarity.

So far, we have talked primarily about conflicts with others. Nevertheless, you reach a greater level of communication when you can address an issue in which the other person has conflict with you. This requires confidence and an ability to be transparent, but it will yield great fruit to the relationship. Sometimes healthy communication includes bringing attention to a possible misunderstanding, while other times it is admitting when you are wrong. Either way, confronting the other person with love and respect when he has an issue with you can let him know that you are approachable. Try asking the other person, "When I said/did _____, how did you feel?" During the Sermon on the Mount, Jesus tells us to go to the one who has something against us:

> *Therefore if you bring your gift to the altar, and there remember that your brother has something against you, leave your gift there before the altar, and go your way. First be reconciled to your brother, and then come and offer your gift.*
>
> — *MATTHEW 5:23-24*

Reflective Listening is a great tool, whether there is conflict or not. When someone comes to you and tells you something, you can use this tool and reflect back what you hear. Two people can experience true love and intimacy when they listen from the heart to each other and reflect concern for the other person more than self.

Proverbs for Healthy Communication

When following the guidelines of this chapter, it is imperative to seek God for wisdom. The book of Proverbs is full of wisdom and speaks directly to interpersonal discord. Here are some proverbs for you to read, meditate on, and apply to your interactions with others:

> *The heart of the righteous studies how to answer,*
>   *But the mouth of the wicked pours forth evil.*

— *PROVERBS 15:28*

> *The preparations of the heart belong to man,*
>   *But the answer of the tongue is from the LORD.*

— *PROVERBS 16:1*

> *Better is a dry morsel with quietness,*
>   *Than a house full of feasting with strife.*

— *PROVERBS 17:1*

> *He who answers a matter before he hears it,*
>   *It is folly and shame to him.*

— *PROVERBS 18:13*

> *Do not speak in the hearing of a fool,*
>   *For he will despise the wisdom of your words.*

— *PROVERBS 23:9*

Prayer

Dear Lord, thank You for creating each of us as unique individuals with our own special purposes. Teach me not to judge other people because they are different, but rather to celebrate our differences. Please guide and direct me when I face conflict, and help me to know when to confront or not to confront, what to say, and what to pray. I especially pray for the ability to hear with understanding and for wisdom to respond accordingly as I seek Your revelation. Help me to see the truth of the conflict rather than just what appears on the surface. Bring peace to my heart and help me to be unified with others so that we can share Your peace with the world. In Jesus' Name, Amen!

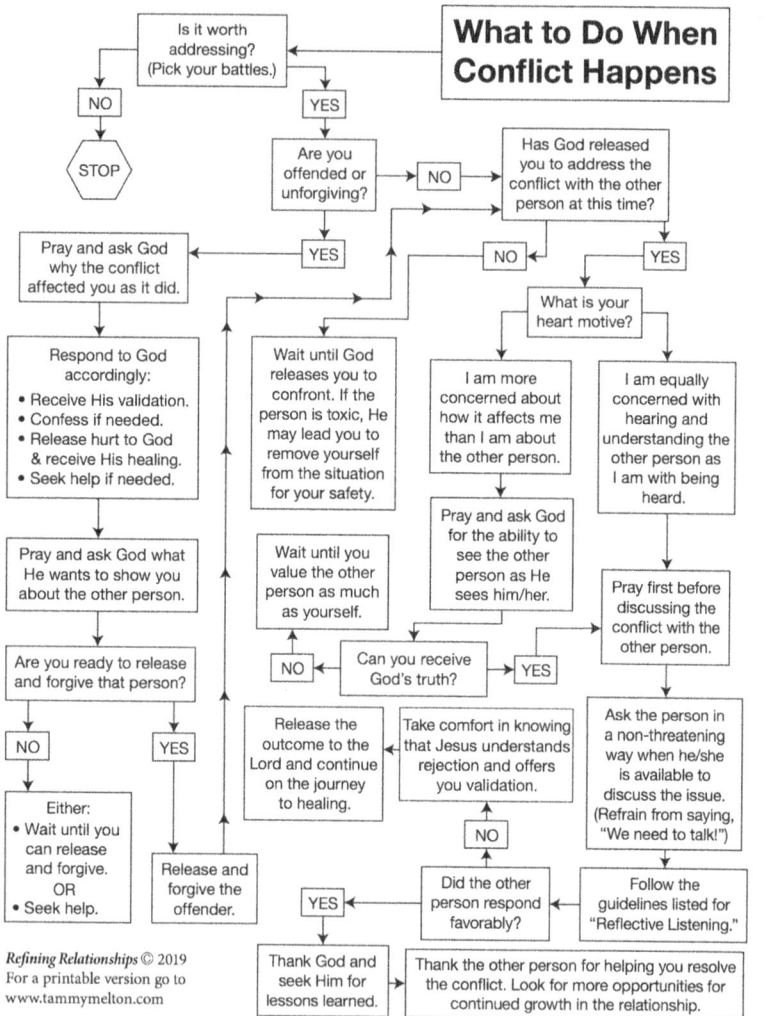

What to Do When Conflict Happens

Is it worth addressing? (Pick your battles.)

NO → STOP

YES → Are you offended or unforgiving?

NO → Has God released you to address the conflict with the other person at this time?

YES → Pray and ask God why the conflict affected you as it did.

Respond to God accordingly:
• Receive His validation.
• Confess if needed.
• Release hurt to God & receive His healing.
• Seek help if needed.

Pray and ask God what He wants to show you about the other person.

Are you ready to release and forgive that person?

NO → Either:
• Wait until you can release and forgive.
OR
• Seek help.

YES → Release and forgive the offender.

Wait until God releases you to confront. If the person is toxic, He may lead you to remove yourself from the situation for your safety.

Wait until you value the other person as much as yourself.

Can you receive God's truth?

NO → Release the outcome to the Lord and continue on the journey to healing.

What is your heart motive?

I am more concerned about how it affects me than I am about the other person.

Pray and ask God for the ability to see the other person as He sees him/her.

I am equally concerned with hearing and understanding the other person as I am with being heard.

Pray first before discussing the conflict with the other person.

Take comfort in knowing that Jesus understands rejection and offers you validation.

YES → Ask the person in a non-threatening way when he/she is available to discuss the issue. (Refrain from saying, "We need to talk!")

Follow the guidelines listed for "Reflective Listening."

Did the other person respond favorably?

NO → (Take comfort in knowing...)

YES → Thank God and seek Him for lessons learned.

Thank the other person for helping you resolve the conflict. Look for more opportunities for continued growth in the relationship.

Refining Relationships © 2019
For a printable version go to
www.tammymelton.com

8

THE DANGER OF ANGER

> *So then, my beloved brethren, let every man be swift to hear,*
> *slow to speak, slow to wrath; for the wrath of man does not*
> *produce the righteousness of God.*
>
> — *JAMES 1:19-20*

A NGER COMES IN many forms. Some people express their frustrations aggressively by yelling accusations and profanity, which can lead to depression and anxiety within the recipients of their fury. As time goes by, many aggressive people carry guilt and condemnation as they reflect and see the damage they have caused in relationships.[1] Other people internalize their anger passively, attempting to hide their anger from others. Unfortunately, this internalization can cause depression and anxiety within themselves. If they are not careful, their pent-up anger can lead to an outburst, surprising their unexpecting friends and family. Whether anger is expressed aggressively or passively, it causes damage inside both the people experiencing anger and their loved ones.

You may be thinking, "I am not aggressive or passive; I must not have an anger issue." Truth be told, all of us have to deal with anger occasionally. Anger is experienced on a wide continuum, ranging from mild irritation to destructive fits of rage. Have you ever taken offense to another person's words or actions? We all have! When we are offended, we are operating in anger. However, anger itself is not sin. The Bible tells that us we can be angry and still not sin:

> Be ye angry, and sin not: let not the sun go down upon your wrath: Neither give place to the devil.
>
> — EPHESIANS 4:26-27 (KJV)

When someone wrongs us, it is normal to be angry. Upon experiencing anger, we need to quickly release our irritations over to God and ask Him for wisdom in dealing with the situation. Otherwise, our wrath can turn into a root of bitterness, negatively affecting us and all those around us.[2] If we hold on to anger too long, we open the door for the enemy to come between us and the ones with whom we are upset. As mentioned in chapter five, Ephesians 4 proceeds to tell us that we can actually grieve the Holy Spirit when we hurt others in our anger.[3]

When Anger is Positive

Sometimes anger is actually a positive attribute. God may allow a bit of righteous indignation to motivate us toward justice. Jesus, who never sinned, had righteous anger when He drove out the money changers in the temple. Notice that Jesus did not merely think angry thoughts, but rather He did something about the injustice; His actions resulted in God's purpose being restored to His temple:

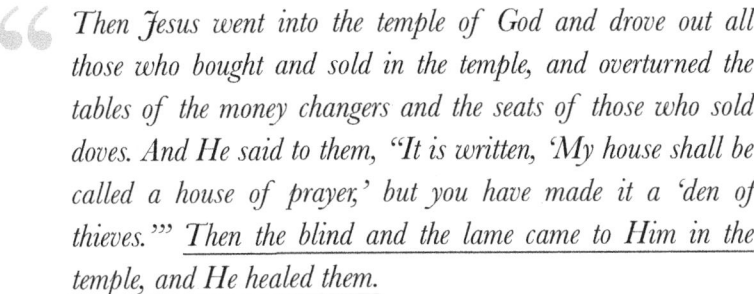

Then Jesus went into the temple of God and drove out all those who bought and sold in the temple, and overturned the tables of the money changers and the seats of those who sold doves. And He said to them, "It is written, 'My house shall be called a house of prayer,' but you have made it a 'den of thieves.'" Then the blind and the lame came to Him in the temple, and He healed them.

— MATTHEW 21:12-14 (EMPHASIS ADDED)

While God allows righteous indignation in order to address injustice, some people call their anger "righteous indignation," when it is anything but righteous. I believe a test of whether anger is righteous indignation or the wrath of man is the motivation of one's heart. If someone is truly considering the good of others, his anger could be from God. However, if he is selfishly thinking about his own rights being violated and is upset because something is not going *his* way, chances are that his anger is what James calls "the wrath of man."[4] This also applies to a parent's discipline of his children. If his heart motive in punishing a child is for the good of the child, it will produce a harvest of righteousness and peace in the child.[5] However, if the parent disciplines his child out of anger, he will then be provoking his child to follow suit with anger.[6]

Even if anger is not intended to help social injustice, it can still be beneficial when it helps alert us about a deeper issue. According to an old metaphor, anger is like a "check engine" light on the dashboard of a car; it alerts you to a problem that needs attention. I tell clients that anger is never the root of anything. More than likely, something deeper is fueling the anger, such as loneliness, abandonment, unforgiveness, etc. These negative emotions must be addressed in order to curb anger meltdowns. Sometimes, especially in the Church, the message is preached to not be led by emotions. We are taught that emotions will lead us astray. While it is true that we often have to proceed with life regardless of how we feel, there comes a time when we need to let God show us why we feel the way we do and stop pretending that "it's all good!"

Adverse Childhood Experiences

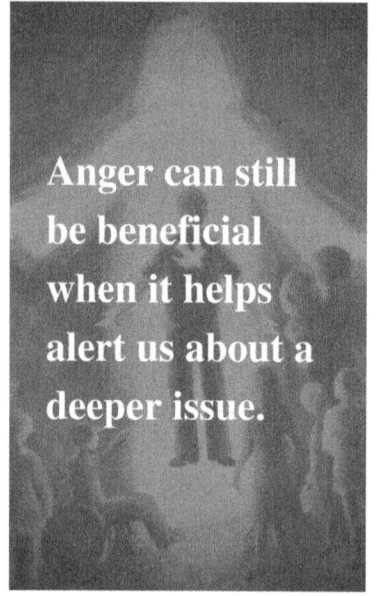

Anger can still be beneficial when it helps alert us about a deeper issue.

Many times the underlying source of anger is rooted in what counselors call adverse childhood experiences (ACE). Traumatic events, such as the divorce of parents, sexual abuse, verbal abuse, and neglect can wreak havoc emotionally, mentally, spiritually, and physically throughout a person's lifetime. When a child experiences these unfortunate events, part of his heart holds on to the pain, while the rest of him chooses to get on with life. As life unfolds, more events will trigger the pain he thought he left behind, resulting in a cycle of despair, frustration, and anger.

In the mid-1990's, The Division of Violence Prevention at the Centers for Disease Control and Prevention (CDC), in partnership with Kaiser Permanente, surveyed thousands of HMO patients. They found that anxiety, depression, and anger in children who have been exposed to high levels of traumatic events lead to a higher risk for disease and even earlier death as adults.[7] According to Felitti, et.al., more results of the study include:

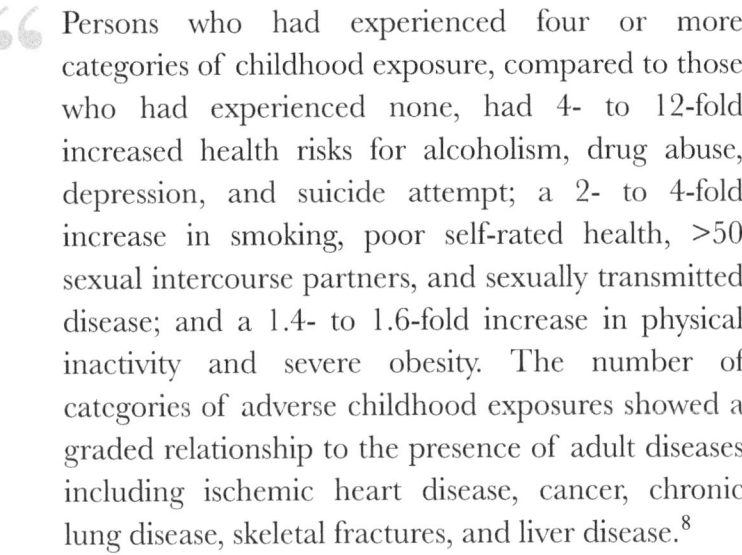

Persons who had experienced four or more categories of childhood exposure, compared to those who had experienced none, had 4- to 12-fold increased health risks for alcoholism, drug abuse, depression, and suicide attempt; a 2- to 4-fold increase in smoking, poor self-rated health, >50 sexual intercourse partners, and sexually transmitted disease; and a 1.4- to 1.6-fold increase in physical inactivity and severe obesity. The number of categories of adverse childhood exposures showed a graded relationship to the presence of adult diseases including ischemic heart disease, cancer, chronic lung disease, skeletal fractures, and liver disease.[8]

In order to clarify examples of traumatic childhood experiences, I have included a copy of the ACE Questionnaire at the end of the chapter.[9, 10] As mentioned in the research above, people who score a four or more (out of ten) have a higher risk for mental and physical ailments in their adult years. In my counseling practice, I suggest that these people attend therapy sessions weekly for an extended period of time.

If left untreated, these deeper roots can cause a person to hurt others. It is true that hurting people hurt other people. However, I believe you can be healed to a degree that protects you from hurt. I like to say, "Hurting people hurt unhealed people." The deeper a person's hurt, the more he will revert to anger as a coping mechanism to "protect" his heart from more hurt. As was mentioned in chapter five, Jesus came to take on our hurts; He does not intend for us to continue holding on to the same pain He already bore. When we allow Him to heal our deep hurts, we will not hurt others with our words and actions as frequently, and we will not be hurt when others lash out against us from their pain.

What to Do When Someone is Angry with You

If a loved one starts spewing out anger, take time to listen to him and validate his feelings rather than taking his outburst personally and being offended. It is hard *not* to take attacks from a loved one personally, especially if you see her offering more grace to others than she does to you. Why would a person who loves you unleash her stress on you? I believe the answer is that the person thinks she can be authentic and release her frustrations because she knows that you love and accept her. This truth does not justify the action; it only sheds light on why one would fight with her loved ones and not argue with casual acquaintances. I remember having an "aha" moment with this truth concerning a personal relationship. The tension in the relationship began to diminish when I stopped taking the other person's actions personally, allowed her to vent, and then validated her feelings.

Think of a time recently when you got irritated and raised your voice in frustration to a loved one. Consider how you would have felt if your loved one responded with the following statements: "I can see that this is really upsetting you. Can you please tell me why this is irritating to you? I really want to understand where you are coming from." I venture to say that your irritation would diminish and you would be more likely to engage in productive communication about what is happening. Unfortunately, we do not respond so calmly in our human nature. More often, the initial response when someone yells at a loved one in anger is to yell back and begin to accuse the person of what *he* is doing wrong. The destructive cycle continues with words like, "Well, you always..." or "You never..." or "Remember the time when you..." STOP! We are not truly communicating when we throw these kinds of accusations back and forth; just talking *at* each other is not healthy conversation. True communication occurs when each person listens and seeks to understand the other person before responding. At their core, people just want to be heard and validated. As mentioned in chapter six, validation does not mean that you have to agree with the person; it just brings understanding to why the person feels the way he does. Empathy then pairs with validation as a tool of reconciliation, instead of division.

Many people stumble at the idea of showing empathy toward a loved one who is taking out anger on them. It seems as though an angry person does not deserve empathy. However, if God uses empathy to heal the person of deeper issues, why not try it? Would you rather detonate the person's anger or help to dismantle it? While it is not your responsibility to change an angry loved one, how you respond to her can either promote her anger or lessen it. Proverbs 15:1 (NLT) says, "A gentle answer deflects anger, but harsh words make tempers flare." If you are still struggling to offer validation to someone during conflict, I encourage you to follow the steps mentioned in the "Spiritual Warfare in Relationships" chapter about releasing and forgiving.

As you allow God to flow through you in this act of reconciliation, you will find that God uses the other person's dysfunction to surface wounds in your life that need to be healed. I believe this is what Solomon meant in Proverbs when he wrote, "As iron sharpens iron, so one person sharpens another."[11] I encourage you to pray and ask God to use the other person to sharpen you, even as a knife is rubbed over and over on a stone in order to become sharp. Don't be surprised if you find yourself thanking God for the conflict because He used it to heal areas in your life that you did not even know needed healing!

When Anger is a Form of Envy and Self-Seeking

When we do not empathize or validate the other person, we are merely operating out of selfish motives. True communication does not occur when validation and empathy are withheld. James calls this "envy and self-seeking":

 Who is wise and understanding among you? Let him show by good conduct that his works are done in the meekness of wisdom. But if you have bitter envy and self-seeking in your hearts, do not boast and lie against the truth. This wisdom does not descend from above, but is earthly, sensual, demonic. For where envy and self-seeking exist, confusion and every evil thing are there.

—JAMES 3:13-16

I recently witnessed this happening between two people at the grocery store. A girl, probably in her 20s, was disrespecting her mother with condescending remarks and a harsh tone of voice without regard to anyone else in the store hearing. I contemplated approaching her and saying, "Excuse me, but do you love your mother?" I was thinking that I would have loved to have those two in my therapy office! I am not sure I really would have approached them, but another customer could not take it anymore and began reprimanding the young lady. Their yelling and cursing soon filled the atmosphere—so much so that people all over the store, from the meat department to the pharmacy, could hear the knock-down, drag-out fight taking place between two strangers. Even as I write this, I find myself praying for all three involved: the lady who jumped in to defend the mother, the girl who started the whole ordeal, and her poor mother who seemed to be disengaged. Sadly, no one "won" and the problem was not solved.

We need to remember that anger, when it is a by-product of selfish motives, is sin. As Christians, we are sometimes quick to point out the danger in other people's sins, such as sexual immorality or drunkenness, but we do not think about our guilt during heated arguments with loved ones. Notice that "outbursts of anger" is right in the middle of a long list of sins listed in the book of Galatians:

 When you follow the desires of your sinful nature, the results are very clear: sexual immorality, impurity, lustful pleasures, idolatry, sorcery, hostility, quarreling, jealousy, outbursts of anger, selfish ambition, dissension, division, envy, drunkenness, wild parties, and other sins like these. Let me tell you again, as I have before, that anyone living that sort of life will not inherit the Kingdom of God.

— GALATIANS *5:19-21 (NLT, EMPHASIS ADDED)*

What to Do About Your Own Anger

If you have an issue with anger, ask yourself why you revert to anger so readily in times of conflict. Is there a "benefit" to acting out in anger? One person told me that she gets angry in order to keep people at arm's length so she will not be hurt again. As was previously mentioned, she was putting up anger like a shield to "protect" herself from hurt; however, her "shield" soon turned into prison bars, keeping her captured in fear and pain. The following are actual answers people gave me to explain what "benefits" they think they will get when they lash out in anger:

- Attention
- Control
- Defense
- Validation
- Respect
- Give the other what he deserves
- Teach the other a lesson
- Make him see my way

A small percentage of my clients are referred to me by the court system in order to go through a mandatory anger management program. The anger management helps clients learn how to cope with anger in practical ways. Although I believe in the inner healing process of getting to root causes of anger, I know that coping skills are also important. Inner healing works from the inside out, while learning about anger management works on the outside in.

It is important to identify what triggers you to get angry. Possible triggers include: being wrongfully accused, being lied to, being late, being held up in traffic, and many other scenarios. When faced with a specific trigger, decide if you can avoid it. If not, ask yourself how you can view the situation in a healthier manner. Also, decide if you can do anything to change the situation. Oftentimes our anger arises because we cannot change our circumstance. The famous "Serenity Prayer" used by Alcoholics Anonymous is a great resource to help in situations that are out of our control:

> God grant us the serenity to accept the things we cannot change, courage to change the things we can, and wisdom to know the difference.[12]

One thing we cannot change is what other people think. Our obsessions with other people's opinions hinder our own inner healing. What difference does it make what someone else thinks of us? The reality is that not everyone is going to like us or approve of everything we do. Remember that they are broken individuals anyway, and their view of us is filtered through their pain and lack of knowing all the details. If you have this problem of worrying about what others think, read and meditate on the following verse:

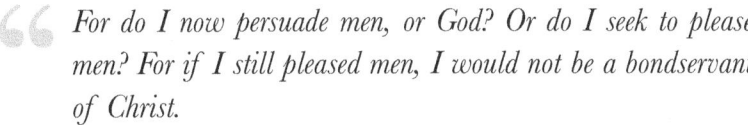

> *For do I now persuade men, or God? Or do I seek to please men? For if I still pleased men, I would not be a bondservant of Christ.*

> — GALATIANS 1:10

Making a Game Plan

There are many tools you can use to manage anger. The first step is to measure how angry you really are. An outrage of anger does not happen suddenly; mild irritations lead to frustrations, which, left unchecked, manifest into an explosion. I use an anger thermometer to teach clients about anger management. These anger thermometers, available from many online sources, use a scale of 1-10, with 1 representing calm and 10 representing an explosive episode of anger. It can be beneficial to look on the thermometer and find that your irritations, unnoticed by others, will lead to a bigger problem of anger if not addressed.

Awareness of personal signs can indicate an upcoming explosion of anger. Most people do not recognize their warning signs. These cues are physical, emotional, behavioral, and cognitive. When you are aware of your own unique signs in these four areas, you can then address them before you take your anger out on others in ways you will regret. Here are some examples of common signs in each of the four areas mentioned:

Physical Signs	Rising body temperature Racing heart beat Muscle tension Headache/stomach ache
Emotional Signs	Fear Anxiety Depression Shame
Behavioral Signs	Raised voice Hitting something Pacing the floor Silent treatment
Cognitive Signs	Negative thoughts: "How dare they...." "No one cares about me." "I'll teach you!"

When you notice that your anger is rising, you can then do

something to prevent continued escalation. Here are just some of the tools you can use to help diffuse your anger:

- Stop and pray. Give the Lord your frustrations and ask for His perspective.
- Remove yourself from the situation for a "time out" to calm down. Be careful not to think of this as running away or giving a silent treatment to the person who is upsetting you. Simply communicate to the person that you need to step away to regroup and that you will be back.
- Take a deep breath through your nose like you are smelling a flower. Hold your breath for a second and then exhale out your mouth like you are blowing out a candle. Repeat this a few times. I like to thank God for His peaceful presence when I inhale and give Him my anxiety on the exhale. While you are taking deep breaths, you can also scan your body and release muscle tension.
- Exercise. Take a walk or do some strength training.
- Journal. You can journal about all that is frustrating you and then write a prayer giving it to God. You can also journal about what you are thankful for to remember that life is not all stressful.
- Hold an imaginary container in your hands. Imagine that you can put all the things that are irritating you into the container, including the situation itself, your anger, anxiety, negative thoughts, etc. What does it feel like to hold the container? What does the container "look" like? Do you feel lighter when you think about having all the irritations in the container instead of inside you? When you are ready, stand up and lift the imaginary container

to the Lord. Trust Him to deal with those things in His timing and ask Him for a different container filled with His unconditional love and guidance.

Now that we know what signs to look for and have tools to help diffuse anger, we can start seeing relationships being refined like never before. I encourage you to surrender your anger to God and see what He can do. What a blessing it is to experience a release from the bondage of anger!

Prayer

Lord, I ask that You give me Your perspective of my anger. Thank You for using it as a warning sign to alert me to deeper issues I need to address. Help us to be aware of my warning signs, and remind me what to do to dissipate my frustrations. Please let me know quickly when I cross the line and fall into the wrath of man rather than righteous indignation. I choose to lay down my weapons and let You defend me.

> *Truly my soul silently waits for God;*
> *From Him comes my salvation.*
> *He only is my rock and my salvation;*
> *He is my defense;*
> *I shall not be greatly moved.*

— *PSALM 62:1-2*

NOTE:

Research such as the study on Adverse Childhood Experiences demonstrates why an emphasis on proper mental health care is so important. The good news is that God can heal these deep wounds from past trauma and actually use them in a person's life to set other people free. Unfortunately, church leaders often neglect to promote the benefits of psychological care; in fact, some even say it is unnecessary, or even evil. Hurting church members are given sermons with scriptures telling them to stop thinking negative thoughts and feeling negative emotions. However, they are not taught how to apply those principles in practical ways. Some of those verses are actually taken out of context, giving the person a wrong message. For example, contrary to many sermons I have heard, the scripture where Paul says that he forgets the things in the past and presses on to the future[13] is not in reference to past traumatic experiences and wounds; rather, it refers to Paul's self-confidence in his fervent pursuit of religion before he became a Christian.[14]

The only way one can truly be set free from the bondages of the past is to allow God to reveal the deepest wound, show His perspective, and heal the inner man. One may say he is forgetting all of his painful past; in reality, those memories are stored in the brain and will pop up at the threat of danger, just like a beachball pressed down under water. When I work with clients who have experienced a traumatic past, I reassure them that the purpose of revisiting

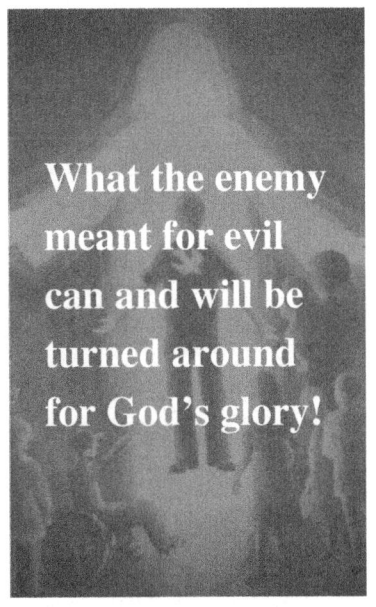

What the enemy meant for evil can and will be turned around for God's glory!

memories is not to retraumatize them but to help them receive God's perspective and freedom. I am careful not to process painful memories when the client is not ready. When they are ready, I remind them that they are safe now; we are, in a sense, just letting God take them by the hand to lead them from a state of brokenness to one of wholeness. What a glorious experience to witness God setting people free to experience His love and purpose for their life at an even deeper level because of the past. What the enemy meant for evil can and *will* be turned around for God's glory when we allow God to transform us from the unhealthy perspectives of our past.

FINDING YOUR ACE (ADVERSE CHILDHOOD EXPERIENCES) SCORE

While you were growing up, during your first 18 years of life:

1. Did a parent or other adult in the household often or very often...

Swear at you, insult you, put you down, or humiliate you?
OR
Act in a way that made you afraid that you might be physically hurt?

Yes or No | If yes, enter 1 _____

2. Did a parent or other adult in the household often or very often...

Push, grab, slap, or throw something at you?
OR
Ever hit you so hard that you had marks or were injured?

Yes or No | If yes, enter 1 _____

3. Did an adult or person at least 5 years older than you ever...

Touch or fondle you or have you touch their body in a sexual way?
OR
Attempt or actually have oral, anal, or vaginal intercourse with you?

Yes or No | If yes, enter 1 _____

4. Did you often or very often feel that...

No one in your family loved you or thought you were important or special?

OR

Your family didn't look out for each other, feel close to each other, or support each other?

Yes or No | If yes, enter 1 _____

5. Did you often or very often feel that...

You didn't have enough to eat, had to wear dirty clothes, and had no one to protect you?

OR

Your parents were too drunk or high to take care of you or take you to the doctor if needed?

Yes or No | If yes, enter 1 _____

6. Were your parents ever separated or divorced?

Yes or No | If yes, enter 1 _____

7. Was your mother or stepmother:

Often or very often pushed, grabbed, slapped, or had something thrown at her?

OR

Sometimes, often, or very often kicked, bitten, hit with a fist, or hit with something hard?

OR

Ever repeatedly hit at least a few minutes or threatened with a gun or knife?

Yes or No | If yes, enter 1 _____

8. Did you live with anyone who was a problem drinker or alcoholic or who used street drugs?

Yes or No | If yes, enter 1 _____

9. Was a household member depressed or mentally ill, or did a household member attempt suicide?

Yes or No | If yes, enter 1 _____

10. Did a household member go to prison?

Yes or No | If yes, enter 1 _____

**Now add up your "Yes" answers: _____
This is your ACE Score.**

JESUS, OUR ULTIMATE EXAMPLE

> *Let this mind be in you which was also in Christ Jesus, who, being in the form of God, did not consider it robbery to be equal with God, but made Himself of no reputation, taking the form of a bondservant, and coming in the likeness of men. And being found in appearance as a man, He humbled Himself and became obedient to the point of death, even the death of the cross. Therefore God also has highly exalted Him and given Him the name which is above every name, that at the name of Jesus every knee should bow, of those in heaven, and of those on earth, and of those under the earth, and that every tongue should confess that Jesus Christ is Lord, to the glory of God the Father.*
>
> *— PHILIPPIANS 2:5-11*

CHRISTIANITY IS UNIQUE among other religions. Believers like to say that Christianity is more about relationship than it is about religion; religion is man's attempt to reach God, but Christianity is God reaching down to man—literally! Jesus left the throne of Heaven and came to earth in human form to pay for the sins of man with His own blood.

Most religions teach that man has to perform good works in order to make it to Heaven. However, the tenants of our faith teach that salvation is a gift of God given to us by grace through faith.[1] What does that mean? Our salvation was paid in full by Jesus' death on the cross. When we acknowledge and accept His gift of salvation, we are free to serve Him out of love and not out of obligation.

Praise be unto God, who gave us such an incredible gift through Jesus Christ! He modeled how to live abundantly, even in the midst of turmoil. The author of Hebrews exhorts us to look to Jesus as our example:

> *... let us run with endurance the race that is set before us, looking unto Jesus, the author and finisher of our faith, who for the joy that was set before Him endured the cross, despising the shame, and has sat down at the right hand of the throne of God. For consider Him who endured such hostility from sinners against Himself, lest you become weary and discouraged in your souls.*
>
> — *HEBREWS 12:1B-3*

Jesus' Example of Humility

James 4:10 exhorts, "Humble yourselves in the sight of the Lord, and He will lift you up." There is no greater example of humility than our Lord, Jesus Christ, who left the splendors of Heaven to become a little baby. Likewise, God wants us to lay down our lives for others, as evident in the following verses:

> *Greater love has no one than this, than to lay down one's life for his friends.*
>
> — JOHN 15:13

> *By this we know love, because He laid down His life for us. And we also ought to lay down our lives for the brethren.*
>
> — 1 JOHN 3:16

> *And whosoever will be chief among you, let him be your servant: Even as the Son of man came not to be ministered unto, but to minister, and to give his life a ransom for many.*
>
> — MATTHEW 20:27-28 (KJV)

In our human nature, we do not automatically put others first. Imagine if we all honored others instead of being so self-absorbed. Talk about transformed relationships! We can only honor others when we abide in Christ and allow Him to honor them through us.[2] As we abide in Him, we will find that He alone can meet our needs. Thus, we will not have a reason for self-pity, and we can then genuinely treat others with respect.

Jesus' Example of Not Defending Himself

When we fail to abide in Christ, we can easily feel like we have to defend and protect ourselves. We especially tend to be defensive when rumors are being spread about us and people falsely accuse us. If anyone understands being falsely accused and misrepresented, it is Jesus. However, He did not defend Himself. Isaiah foretold of His suffering and said:

> *He was oppressed and He was afflicted,*
> *Yet He opened not His mouth;*
> *He was led as a lamb to the slaughter,*
> *And as a sheep before its shearers is silent,*
> *So He opened not His mouth.*
>
> — Isaiah 53:7 (emphasis added)

This prophecy was fulfilled right before the crucifixion when Jesus was taken to stand trial before the Roman authorities:

> *Now Jesus stood before the governor. And the governor asked Him, saying, "Are You the King of the Jews?" Jesus said to him, "It is as you say." And while He was being accused by the chief priests and elders, He answered nothing. Then Pilate said to Him, "Do You not hear how many things they testify against You?" But He answered him not one word, so that the governor marveled greatly.*
>
> — Matthew 27:11-13 (emphasis added)

Not only did Jesus not defend Himself, but he also did not need anyone else to defend Him. When Jesus was arrested to be taken to trial, Peter rose up to defend Him and actually cut off the ear of a Roman soldier:

> *But Jesus said to him, "Put your sword in its place, for all who take the sword will perish by the sword. Or do you think that I cannot now pray to My Father, and He will provide Me with more than twelve legions of angels? How then could the Scriptures be fulfilled, that it must happen thus?"*
>
> — Matthew 26:52-54

Jesus knew that God ordained His suffering so that we could be reconciled to Him. Though agonizing, the cross was required in order to pay the price for the sins of all mankind. However, Jesus' death would have been in vain if He did not leave the grave; on the third day, Jesus conquered death when He was resurrected from the dead! What more could He conquer than death? No other religion can say that their leader resurrected from the dead.

Jesus' Example of Defending His Beloved

The Good News is that because of the Resurrection, Jesus is alive and ready to defend us; we do not need to defend ourselves or look to anyone else to defend us. Jesus is present not just to defend us, but to reveal Himself through our trials as a testimony to others. When the Apostle John was taken in exile to die on the Isle of Patmos, the resurrected Jesus appeared to him! Jesus did not just appear for John's sake, but He came to reveal His Revelation through John to us. John writes:

> *And when I saw Him, I fell at His feet as dead. But He laid His right hand on me, saying to me, "Do not be afraid; I am the First and the Last. I am He who lives, and was dead, and behold, I am alive forevermore. Amen. And I have the keys of Hades and of Death."*

> — *REVELATION 1:17-18*

Another example of Jesus arriving to protect someone is found in the Old Testament with Shadrack, Meshack, and Abed-Nego. While the Hebrews were held captive by the Babylonians, a decree was made that everyone had to bow down to the golden image of the king. These three Hebrew men worshipped the true

Almighty God and refused to bow down to any other god. Consequently, they were taken to the king to face trial. The king warned them that if they did not bow down to the idol, they would be thrown into a fiery furnace to die. They responded:

> *"O Nebuchadnezzar, we have no need to answer you in this matter. If that is the case, our God whom we serve is able to deliver us from the burning fiery furnace, and He will deliver us from your hand, O king. But if not, let it be known to you, O king, that we do not serve your gods, nor will we worship the gold image which you have set up."*
>
> — *DANIEL 3:16-18*

They were indeed bound up and thrown into the fire, but God rescued them so thoroughly that when they were taken out of the fire, they did not even smell like smoke! Their confident act of faith was rewarded with the pre-incarnate Christ actually visiting them in the fire!

> *Then King Nebuchadnezzar was astonished; and he rose in haste and spoke, saying to his counselors, "Did we not cast three men bound into the midst of the fire?"*
>
> *They answered and said to the king, "True, O king."*
>
> *"Look!" he answered, "I see four men loose, walking in the midst of the fire; and they are not hurt, and the form of the fourth is like the Son of God."*
>
> — *DANIEL 3: 24-25*

Jesus' Example of Prayer and Surrendering His Will to the Father

Shadrach, Meshach, and Abed-Nego must have learned what Jesus taught us about the importance of praying and surrendering our will to God. Before Jesus' trial and crucifixion, He spent hours in the Garden of Gethsemane surrendering His will to the Father. Luke's rendition of the events showed that Jesus "was accustomed" to pulling away to pray. He modeled a life of prayer for his disciples and taught them that prayer is vitally important in combating temptation:

> *Coming out, He went to the Mount of Olives, as He was accustomed, and His disciples also followed Him. When He came to the place, He said to them, "Pray that you may not enter into temptation."*
>
> *And He was withdrawn from them about a stone's throw, and He knelt down and prayed, saying, "Father, if it is Your will, take this cup away from Me; nevertheless not My will, but Yours, be done." Then an angel appeared to Him from heaven, strengthening Him. And being in agony, He prayed more earnestly. Then His sweat became like great drops of blood falling down to the ground.*
>
> *When He rose up from prayer, and had come to His disciples, He found them sleeping from sorrow. Then He said to them, "Why do you sleep? Rise and pray, lest you enter into temptation."*
>
> — *Luke 22:39-46*

Jesus did not give in to the temptation to defend himself in front of the Roman authorities because he had already prepared Himself in prayer. You may say, "Well, Jesus was God. I am not."

True. However, He was also fully human in order to pay for human sins. The author of Hebrews addresses this:

> *For we do not have a High Priest who cannot sympathize with our weaknesses, but was in all points tempted as we are, yet without sin.*

— *Hebrews 4:15*

Being tempted is not a sin; following through with the temptation is sin. Many people lose heart with temptations, but they forget that Jesus, who was also tempted yet never sinned, models the way out of temptation.[3] We do not have to enter the enemy's downward spiral of temptation, sin, more temptation, and more sin. I once heard someone say that when he spent time with God, he was not tempted to look at porn, but when he neglected prayer, worship, and Bible study, he found himself lured into the downward cycle again. As we spend time with God, He purifies our desires by aligning them to His own; He then takes pleasure in giving us the desires of our hearts.[4] How exciting to look back and see that previous temptations are not tempting anymore because God is developing purity within us! Jesus told his disciples in the Sermon on the Mount that the pure in heart will see God.[5] When we see Him, we are able to follow Him more clearly and can trade our downward cycle of temp-

Jesus did not give in to the temptation to defend himself because he had already prepared Himself in prayer.

tation and sin for an upward cycle of purity and Christ-likeness.

Jesus' Example of Intimacy in Relationships

Jesus' custom of pulling away from the crowds and getting alone with the Father showed the importance of pursuing an intimate relationship with God. We see an example of this in the book of Mark:

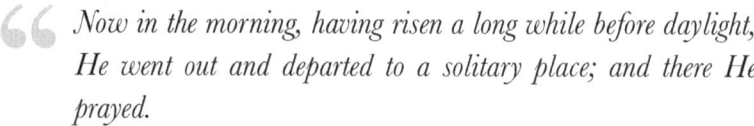

> *Now in the morning, having risen a long while before daylight, He went out and departed to a solitary place; and there He prayed.*

> — *MARK 1:35*

If Jesus needed time alone with the Father in prayer, how much more do we? As we spend time with God, not only do we overcome temptation, but we also gain the wisdom needed to know what level of intimacy to have with others.

Jesus had different levels of intimacy with people around Him when He was on this earth. He had compassion on the multitudes; He trained and sent out seventy to minister in the community; He poured into the lives of twelve disciples; He invested a significant amount of His time in an inner circle with three of His disciples; and He spent quality time alone with One: the Father. Likewise, we need seek God for the level of intimacy we can share with the people in our lives; we can cause more harm than good if we share intimate information with a casual acquaintance rather than with someone we know and trust in our inner circle. In this way, we can be transparent, yet protected, knowing that our intimacy with the One will give us wisdom in dealing with all other relationships.

Jesus' Example of Not Being Affected by Expectations

Jesus did not have unrealistic expectations on people. The Bible tells us of a time when many people believed in Jesus after they saw Him perform miracles. However, He was not swayed by their accolades, because He knew what was in their hearts:

> *Now when He was in Jerusalem at the Passover, during the feast, many believed in His name when they saw the signs which He did. But Jesus did not commit Himself to them, because He knew all men, and had no need that anyone should testify of man, for He knew what was in man.*
>
> — *JOHN 2:23-25*

Jesus did not expect them to act differently from what He knew was in their hearts. Even so, He still loved them, as His love for people was the reason He came to earth. Jesus also did not wait until they changed to love them. Romans 5:8 says, "But God demonstrates His own love toward us, in that while we were still sinners, Christ died for us." Why do we tend to withhold our love from people who do not meet our expectations? We want to wait until they "act right" to love them. Maybe people will be influenced to make positive changes if we follow Christ's example and love them even before they are transformed.

Not only did Jesus avoid holding unrealistic expectations over people, but He was also not bound by what other people thought He should do. We know this from when He heard that his good friend, Lazarus, was sick. Lazarus' sisters wanted Jesus to come. They may have even tried to manipulate Him when they sent a message saying, "Lord, behold, he whom You love is sick."[6] Jesus waited two more days before going, during which time Lazarus died. When He arrived, Lazarus' sister, Martha, blamed Jesus,

"Lord, if You had been here, my brother would not have died."[7] Jesus was not moved by her accusation. He proceeded to actually raise Lazarus from the dead. If Jesus had been moved by their expectations of Him to come when Lazarus was sick, they would not have experienced the bigger miracle of their brother being raised from the dead. Likewise, if Jesus had taken offense when Martha blamed Him for her brother's death, He probably would not have raised Lazarus from the dead.

What a great example Christ is to us in how to navigate relationships! No wonder Paul told the Corinthians to follow him as he followed Christ.[8] I pray that you will consider all these examples of Christ's interactions with other people and be encouraged, since that same Christ lives in you if you have surrendered your life to Him.

> *May the God who gives endurance and encouragement give you the same attitude of mind toward each other that Christ Jesus had, so that with one mind and one voice you may glorify the God and Father of our Lord Jesus Christ.*
>
> — ROMANS 15:5-6 (NIV)

Prayer

Thank you, Lord Jesus, for not just telling me how to live, but for being a living example. Thank You for leaving the throne of Heaven to come to earth as a man to rescue me. I need Your help to remember not to be so self-absorbed, merely thinking about my own needs instead of truly caring about other people. Help me to trust You to take care of my needs so that I do not continue to have unrealistic expectations on others. I also want to follow Your example and not be swayed by people's expectations on me when You have assured me of what You want me to do.

Since I operate out of the flesh when I do not look to You, I choose to "put on the Lord Jesus Christ, and make no provision for the flesh, to fulfill its lusts".[9] I look forward to seeing how following Your example will help to refine my relationships! In Jesus' Name, Amen!

ONE WISH

ONE WISH IS a simple, non-threatening method to introduce someone to Jesus, written by Richard Sharp, missionary with Operation Mobilization. One Wish includes two questions and four pictures.

Question One:

If you had one wish from God to you today, what would it be? (Proceed by asking if you can say a brief, one-sentence prayer about the person's one wish.)

Question Two:

Did you know that God has one wish for you? His one wish for you is to be your friend. (Continue by asking the person if you can show him these four pictures.)

A diamond represents how special you and I are to God. He created us and loves us unconditionally. No one is a mistake!

This picture has a dark side and a light side. Do you ever feel like God may be out there somewhere, but He seems so distant? I have felt that way before. The reason is because we have done things

wrong, and God is perfect; our wrongdoings separate us from a holy God.

- Have you ever told a lie? I know I have. That makes us liars.
- Have you ever taken something that did not belong to you? I have. That makes us thieves.
- Have you ever had bitterness against someone and wished he was out of your life? I have. Though we probably would never think of killing him, in our hearts we want him out of our lives as if he was dead. That is like murder.

 Though our sins separate us from God for eternity, God made a plan to reconcile us to Him. God sent His perfect Son Jesus to earth to pay the price for our offenses. This picture of a hand represents Jesus nailed to the cross. (*Take your right hand and hold it out palm up. Get something to represent our sins, such as a phone and place it on your right hand.*) This hand represents you and me, and this phone represents all the wrongs we have ever done. The weight of every lie we have ever told and every item we have ever stolen is on us. God put all our sins on Him (*Transfer the phone onto your left hand.*), and He paid for them with His blood on the cross. Not only did he die a cruel death on the cross, but He conquered death by raising from the dead on the third day, and He still lives today! His death and resurrection free us up to be united with God and start a friendship with Him. (Extend your hand like you are going to shake his hand.)

This picture represents God extending His hand to invite us to be His friend. Would you like to be united with God? If so, you can repeat after me, either out loud or in your heart.

Prayer of Salvation:

God, **I am sorry** for all the wrongs I have done.

Thank You for paying the price for all my sins.

Please **forgive me** of all my sins and come into my life. I want to be your friend.

Encourage the person you lead to the Lord to read the Bible, starting in the book of John, and to find a Bible-believing church where he can get connected and grow in the faith. If you are in a position to disciple him, invite him to meet and go through the scriptures with you. Encourage him to be baptized in water as a sign of his commitment to Christ. Go to www.onewish4you.com for resources to help disciple new believers. Resources include bracelets with the four pictures, as well as friendship booklets with scriptures from the book of John. Richard Sharp is also available to speak for evangelism training and outreach events.

ACKNOWLEDGEMENTS

I WANT TO first thank God for teaching me the principles in this book and for allowing me the opportunity to communicate these truths to others. Lord, I stand amazed at how You have brought together all the details throughout the process of writing and publishing this book. I give You all the glory!

Thank you to Dr. Bob Swanger and the Board of Elders of Harvest Network International for recognizing God's call on my life and for allowing me to network with HNI. I am so grateful to be commissioned through an organization that comes together in unity to spread the Gospel of Jesus Christ to the world!

To my immediate family, Bill, Amy, and Amber: I could not do what I do without you! Amy and Amber, thank you for sharing the light of Jesus so beautifully with others and for your love and prayers for me. Bill, this page cannot contain the words for how grateful I am for you! Thank you for being steadfast in your own walk with God and being my covering as the head of our household. You not only allow me to go forward in my call as a woman in ministry, but you sacrifice in so many ways to bring our dreams to pass. I love you!

I am so grateful to my extended family for all of their love, support, and prayer throughout the years and especially throughout this endeavor. Dad and Mom (Don and Lorene Barron), I love you, and I gratefully take the torch you have passed down to share Christ's love with others!

To the person who was the most involved in helping me write this book, Amy Melton: What a blessing to have you as my editor! I treasure the mom/daughter moments I had with you during hours of getting just the right words down on paper. Thank you for your patience! Who else could have said, "Mom, what are you really trying to say here?" and then proceed to help me clarify the things of my heart into writing? You are truly a gifted communicator!

Thank you to my friends and supporters of Legacy Ministries. I especially appreciate Theresa Simoneau for keeping things organized and allowing me to have more time to plan, write, and counsel. To all past and current board members of Legacy: Thank you for backing me in all I do. Thank you also to the members of the Legacy Ministries Kingdom Speakers and Kingdom Writers groups for continuously encouraging me to keep writing.

God has put a "gutter guard" prayer team into place! Thank you Johanne, Tracy, Theresa, Vicki, Karen, Judy M, Judy R., Vera, Pat, Barbara, Amy, Gail, Jenna, Lori, Brenda, Dusty, Beth, Terri, Sandee, Nancy, Heddie, Arthurine, Melanie and more. Thank you especially to Beth and Terri for not only praying, but also for helping with extra proofreading and edit suggestions.

I would be remiss not to take this opportunity to thank all my past and present clients. Thank you for trusting me to walk alongside you through some of life's most difficult trials. What a privilege it has been to have a front row seat to God's work in your lives! I am also amazed at how God has transformed my own life through things I have learned from all of you.

Thank you to the two people who helped make this book an incredible work of art. Dee Keller, you are in incredible artist! I prayed that people would be drawn to Christ just by seeing the cover, and I think your picture does just that!

Jason Sisam, thank you for your great work in formatting the book and designing the cover. Also, I can't thank you enough for rescuing me from my publishing woes! Your expertise is invaluable!

The picture on the cover of the book was painted by Dee Keller, artist and founder of *Deesigns* For more information about purchasing Dee's artwork, visit https://www.facebook.com/deesigns.stencils, or email her at deekellersmail@yahoo.com.

ⒿⒷ JBSISAM™

For more information about getting your book written and published, contact Jason Sisam by visiting www.jbsisam.com or www.livinglightsmedia.com to see samples of his work.

NOTES

Introduction

1. "Refine," Cambridge University Press, accessed September 22, 2018, https://dictionary.cambridge.org/us/dictionary/english/refine.

1. The Power of Perspective in Relationships

1. "Perspective," Dictionary.com, accessed May 7, 2019, https://www.dictionary.com/browse/perspective.
2. Ephesians 2:14 (NLT)
3. Ephesians 2:22
4. See Matthew 20:26
5. See Matthew 16:25
6. See Jeremiah 1:10 (NIV)
7. See Jeremiah 29:4.
8. See Romans 8:28.
9. See Romans 8:10 and 2 Cor. 5:21.
10. See Zechariah 3:1.
11. See Matthew 4:1.
12. John 8:44.
13. See Revelation 12:10.

2. Refining a Relationship with God

1. See Romans 3:23 and 6:23.
2. See 2 Corinthians 5:21.
3. See Matthew 28:5-6.
4. See Acts 4:12.
5. See John 3:16.
6. See Hebrews 12:1-2.
7. See John 14:16-17; 25-26
8. See Psalm 16:11
9. See John 16:33
10. See 1 John 4:19
11. See Matthew 22:37
12. "Lexicon::Strong's G2588 - *kardia*," Blue Letter Bible, accessed July 7, 2018,

https://www.blueletterbible.org/lang/lexicon/lexicon.cfm?Strongs=
G2588&t=KJV.

13. Eric Metaxas, *Seven Women and the Secret of their Greatness* (Nashville: Nelson Books, 2016), 41.

14. See John 10:11-14.

15. See John 10:27.

16. "This Week's Shocking Stat," Revival Outside the Walls, accessed January 31, 2019,
   https://www.rotw.com/this-weeks-shocking-stat.

17. Ibid.

18. "Behaviors," Revival Outside the Walls, accessed January 31, 2019, https://www.rotw.com/get-facts/behaviors.

19. Ibid.

20. Ibid.

21. Ibid.

22. See Matthew 28:18-20.

23. See also Matthew 10:32-33.

24. Amy Morin, "7 Scientifically Proven Benefits of Gratitude," accessed February 2, 2019, https://www.psychologytoday.com/us/blog/what-mentally-strong-people-dont-do/201504/7-scientifically-proven-benefits-gratitude.

25. See Genesis 14:18-20.

26. Matthew 6:32b-33.

27. See Romans 3:23 and Zephaniah 3:5.

28. See Philippians 4:6-7 and Isaiah 9:6.

29. See 1 Peter 5:7.

3. Refining a Relationship with Self

1. See Matthew 22:37-39.

2. See Matthew 22:40.

3. See Romans 12:3.

4. See Romans 12:10.

5. Hebrews 13:5

6. See Ephesians 4:31-32.

7. Mayo Clinic Staff, "Chronic stress puts your health at risk," accessed February 19, 2019, https://www.mayoclinic.org/healthy-lifestyle/stress-management/in-depth/stress/art-20046037.

8. University of Texas Health Science Center at San Antonio, "Stress can impair memory, reduce brain size in middle age," October 25, 2018, accessed February 9, 2019 https://www.sciencedaily.com/releases/2018/10/181025084043.htm.

9. U.S. Department of Health and Human Services and U.S. Department of Agriculture, *2015 – 2020 Dietary Guidelines for Americans*. 8th Edition. December 2015. Available at https://health.gov/dietaryguidelines/2015/guidelines/, p. vii.

10. "Too Much Can Make Us Sick," University of California, San Francisco, accessed February 13, 2019, http://sugarscience.ucsf.edu/too-much-can-make-us-sick/#.XGQQCyMrI0o.

11. "How Much Is Too Much?," University of California, San Francisco, assessed February 13, 2019, http://sugarscience.ucsf.edu/the-growing-concern-of-overconsumption.html#.XGQROCMrI0o.

12. "Added Sugars," American Stroke Association, accessed on February 13, 2019, https://www.strokeassociation.org/en/healthy-living/healthy-eating/eat-smart/sugar/added-sugars.

13. Ibid.

14. "Children should eat less than 25 grams of sugars daily," American Heart Association, accessed February 13, 2019. http://newsroom.heart.org/news/children-should-eat-less-than-25-grams-of-added-sugars-daily.

15. Ibid.

16. Jeff Iliff, "One more reason to get a good night's sleep," published Oct 13, 2014, accessed February 16, 2019, https://youtu.be/MJK-dMlATmM.

17. Dr. Dan Robotham, Lauren Chakkalackal and Dr. Eva Cyhlarova, *Sleep Matters: The impact of sleep on health and wellbeing,* (London: Mental Health Foundation, London, 2011), 33, accessed February 25, 2019, https://www.mentalhealth.org.uk/sites/default/files/MHF-Sleep-Report-2011.pdf.

18. Zlatan Krizan and Garrett Hisler, "Sleepy Anger: Restricted Sleep Amplifies Angry Feelings," (2018), accessed February 15, 2019, https://www.researchgate.net/publication/327582029_Sleepy_Anger_Restricted_Sleep_Amplifies_Angry_Feelings

19. U.S. Department of Transportation, "Drowsy Driving 2015", 1, accessed February 25, 2019 https://crashstats.nhtsa.dot.gov/Api/Public/ViewPublication/812446.

20. See Proverbs 6:9.

21. Francesco Cappuccio, Lanfranco D'Elia, Pasquale Strazzullo, and Michelle Miller. (2010), "Sleep Duration and All-Cause Mortality: A Systematic Review and Meta-Analysis of Prospective Studies. Sleep. 33. 585-92. 10.1093/sleep/33.5.585, accessed February 21, 2019, https://www.researchgate.net/publication/44599220_Sleep_Duration_and_All-Cause_Mortality_A_Systematic_Review_and_Meta-Analysis_of_Prospective_Studies.

22. U.S. Department of Health and Human Services. *Physical Activity Guidelines for Americans, 2nd edition,* 28, accessed February 19, 2019 https://health.gov/paguidelines/second-edition/pdf/Physical_Activity_Guidelines_2nd_edition.pdf.

23. Ibid., p. 57.

24. See 1 John 1:9.

25. Quentin Fotrell, "The sad reason half of Americans don't take their paid vacation," May 28, 2018, accessed February 20, 2019, https://www.marketwatch.com/story/55-of-american-workers-dont-take-all-their-paid-vacation-2016-06-15.

26. Exodus 20:8

27. See James 4:10.
28. Alan D. Wright, *Free Yourself Be Yourself,* (Colorado Springs: Multnomah Books, 2010), back cover.
29. See Ephesians 4:26.
30. Denise Dillon, "Woman arrested over McDonald's apple pie," February 22, 2019, http://www.fox4news.com/trending/woman-arrested-over-mcdonald-s-apple-pie.

4. Refining Relationships with Others

1. Blake Eastman, "How much of communication is really nonverbal?", accessed February 28, 2019, http://www.nonverbalgroup.com/2011/08/how-much-of-communication-is-really-nonverbal.
2. Barna Group, "Silent and Solo: How Americans Pray", August 15, 2017, accessed March 2, 2019, https://www.barna.com/research/silent-solo-americans-pray/.
3. Ed Stetzer, "New Research: Churchgoers Believe in Sharing Faith, But Most Never Do", August 13, 2012, accessed January 31, 2019, https://www.christianitytoday.com/edstetzer/2012/august/new-research-churchgoers-believe-in-sharing-faith-but-most.html.
4. See 1 Corinthians 13:4.
5. See Exodus 20:17.
6. See Galatians 6:7.
7. See Matthew 7:1.
8. Alex Shashkevich, "Stanford researcher examines how people perceive interruptions in conversation", May 2, 2018, accessed March 4, 2019, https://news.stanford.edu/2018/05/02/exploring-interruption-conversation/.
9. See 1 Corinthians 13:5 (NIV).
10. R.T. Kendall, *Total Forgiveness* (Lake Mary, FL: Charisma House, 2007).
11. Bruce and Toni Hebel, *Forgiving Forward* (Fayetteville, GA: Regenerating Life Press, 2011).
12. See Psalm 91.

5. Spiritual Warfare in Relationships

1. See Ephesians 6:12.
2. See Hebrews 4:12.
3. See John 8:44.
4. See Romans 8:37.
5. John 8:32.

6. Hidden Expectations

1. See Hebrews 12:2.
2. See Psalm 139:23-24.
3. Bruce and Toni Hebel, *Forgiving Forward* (Fayetteville, GA: Regenerating Life Press, 2011), p. 123.
4. See 1 John 5:14.
5. See John 3:30.
6. See Hebrews 13:5b.
7. See Romans 8:28.

7. Dealing with Conflict

1. See Psalm 133:3
2. See Isaiah 53:6
3. See James 1:19.
4. See John 3:17 and Romans 8:1.
5. See James 1:19.

8. The Danger of Anger

1. A person with Narcissistic Personality Disorder (NPD) or Borderline Personality Disorder (BPD) will generally not agree that he has done anything wrong and will blame anyone else but himself for problems in a relationship. However, even someone with NPD or BPD can be helped to be aware of their own anger cues and learn what to do to help.
2. See Hebrews 12:15.
3. See Ephesians 4:30.
4. See James 1:20.
5. See Hebrews 12:11.
6. See Ephesians 6:4.
7. Vincent J. Felitti, MD, FACP et al., "Relationship of Childhood Abuse and Household Dysfunction to Many of the Leading Causes of Death in Adults: The Adverse Childhood Experiences (ACE) Study," *American Journal of Preventive Medicine* 14, no. 4 (1998): 245-258, https://www.ajpmonline.org/article/S0749-3797(98)00017-8/pdf.
8. Ibid., 245.
9. According to the CDC, the use of the ACE Questionnaire is free to use without cost as noted on their website accessed 12/21/18, https://www.cdc.gov/violenceprevention/acestudy/about.html.
10. "Adverse Childhood Experience (ACE) Questionnaire," National Council of Juvenile and Family Court Judges, accessed 12/31/18, https://www.ncjfcj.org/sites/default/files/Finding%20Your%20ACE%20Score.pdf.

11. Proverbs 27:17 (NIV).
12. "The Origin of Our Serenity Prayer," AA History and Trivia, accessed October 31, 2018, http://www.aahistory.com/prayer.html.
13. See Philippians 3:13.
14. See Philippians 3:4-10.

9. Jesus, Our Ultimate Example

1. See Ephesians 2:8-9.
2. See John 15:5
3. See 1 Corinthians 10:13.
4. See Psalm 37:4.
5. See Matthew 5:8.
6. John 11:3 (emphasis added)
7. John 11:21
8. See 1 Corinthians 11:1.
9. Romans 13:14

BIBLIOGRAPHY

American Heart Association. "Children should consume less than 25 grams of sugars daily." Accessed February 13, 2019. http://newsroom.heart.org/news/children-should-eat-less-than-25-grams-of-added-sugars-daily.

American Stroke Association. "Added Sugars." Accessed February 13, 2019. https://www.strokeassociation.org/en/healthy-living/healthy-eating/eat-smart/sugar/added-sugars.

Blue Letter Bible. "Lexicon::Strong's G2588 - *kardia.*" Accessed July 7, 2018. https://www.blueletterbible.org/lang/lexicon/lexicon.cfm?Strongs=G2588&t=KJV

Cambridge University Press. "Refine." Accessed September 22, 2018. https://dictionary.cambridge.org/us/dictionary/english/refine.

Cappuccio, Francesco & D'Elia, Lanfranco & Strazzullo, Pasquale & Miller, Michelle. (2010). Sleep Duration and All-Cause Mortality: A Systematic Review and Meta-Analysis of Prospective Studies. Sleep. 33. 585-92. 10.1093/sleep/33.5.585. Accessed February 21, 2019. https://www.researchgate.net/publication/44599220_Sleep_Duration_and_All-Cause_Mortality_A_Systematic_Review_and_Meta-Analysis_of_Prospective_Studies

Dictionary.com. "Perspective." Accessed May 7, 2019. https://www.dictionary.com/browse/perspective.

Dillon, Denise . "Woman arrested over McDonald's apple pie," February 22, 2019, http://www.fox4news.com/trending/woman-arrested-over-mcdonald-s-apple-pie.

Eastman, Blake. "How much of communication is really nonverbal?". Accessed February 28, 2019. http://www.nonverbalgroup.com/2011/08/how-much-of-communication-is-really-nonverbal.

Felitti, Vincent J., MD, FACP, Robert F. Anda, MD, MS, Dale Nordenberg, MD, David F. Williamson, MS, PhD, Alison M. Spitz, MS, MPH, Valerie Edwards, BA, Mary P. Koss, PhD, and James S. Marks, MD, MPH. "Relationship of Childhood Abuse and Household Dysfunction to Many of the Leading Causes of Death in Adults: The Adverse Childhood Experiences (ACE) Study," *American Journal of Preventive Medicine* 14, no. 4 (1998): 245-258. https://www.ajpmonline.org/article/S0749-3797(98)00017-8/pdf.

Fotrell, Quentin . "The sad reason half of Americans don't take their paid vacation." Market Watch: May 28, 2018. Accessed February 20, 2019, https://www.marketwatch.com/story/55-of-american-workers-dont-take-all-their-paid-vacation-2016-06-15.

Iliff, Jeff. "One more reason to get a good night's sleep." Published October 13, 2014. Accessed February 16, 2019. Video, 11:45. https://www.youtube.com/watch?v=MJK-dMlATmM&feature=youtu.be.

Krizan, Zlatan and Hisler, Garrett. (2018). "Sleepy Anger: Restricted Sleep Amplifies Angry Feelings." Journal of Experi-

mental Psychology General. 10.1037/xgc0000522. Accessed
February 25, 2019.
https://www.researchgate.net/publication/327582029_Sleep-
y_Anger_Restricted_Sleep_Amplifies_Angry_Feelings.

Mayo Foundation for Medical Education and Research
(MFMER). "Chronic stress puts your health at risk."
Accessed February 19, 2019. https://www.mayoclinic.org/
healthy-lifestyle/stress-management/in-depth/stress/art-
20046037

Metaxas, Eric. *Seven Women and the Secret of their Greatness* (Gradu-
ate's Edition). Nashville: Nelson Books, 2016

Morin, Amy. "7 Scientifically Proven Benefits of Gratitude."
Accessed February 2, 2019,
https://www.psychologytoday.com/us/blog/what-mentally-
strong-people-dont-do/201504/7-scientifically-proven-benefits-
gratitude.

National Council of Juvenile and Family Court Judges. "Adverse
Childhood Experience (ACE) Questionnaire." Accessed
December 31, 2018.

Revival Outside the Walls. "Behaviors." Accessed January, 31,
2019. https://www.rotw.com/get-facts/behaviors

Revival Outside the Walls. "This Week's Shocking Stat."
Accessed January 31, 2019. https://www.rotw.com/this-weeks-
shocking-stat.

Robotham, Dr. Dan, Chakkalackal, Lauren and Cyhlarova, Dr.
Eva. *Sleep Matters: The impact of sleep on health and wellbeing.* London:

Mental Health Foundation, London, 2011. Accessed February 25, 2019. https://www.mentalhealth.org.uk/sites/default/files/ MHF-Sleep-Report-2011.pdf.

Shashkevich, Alex. "Stanford researcher examines how people perceive interruptions in conversation". May 2, 2018, Accessed March 4, 2019. https://news.stanford.edu/2018/05/02/ exploring-interruption-conversation/.

University of California San Francisco. "Too Much Can Make Us Sick."Accessed February 13, 2019. http://sugarscience.ucsf. edu/too-much-can-make-us-sick/#.XGQQCyMrI0o.

University of California, San Francisco. "How Much Is Too Much?." Assessed February 13, 2019. http://sugarscience.ucsf. edu/the-growing-concern-of-overconsumption. html#.XGQROCMrI0o.

University of Texas Health Science Center at San Antonio. "Stress can impair memory, reduce brain size in middle age," October 25, 2018. Accessed February 9, 2019. https://www. sciencedaily.com/releases/2018/10/181025084043.htm.

U.S. Department of Health and Human Services and U.S. Department of Agriculture. *2015 – 2020 Dietary Guidelines for Americans*. 8th Edition. December 2015. Available at https:// health.gov/dietaryguidelines/2015/guidelines/.

U.S. Department of Health and Human Services. Physical Activity Guidelines for Americans, 2nd edition. Washington, DC: U.S. Department of Health and Human Services; 2018. Accessed February 19, 2019

U.S. Department of Transportation. "Drowsy Driving 2015." Accessed February 25, 2019. https://crashstats.nhtsa.dot.gov/Api/Public/ViewPublication/812446.

Wright, Alan D. *Free Yourself Be Yourself.* Colorado Springs: Multnomah Books, 2010.

Tammy Melton, LPC has over thirty years of experience working with people as an educator, minister, and licensed professional counselor. Tammy holds ministerial credentials with *Harvest Network International* and is the founder of *Legacy Ministries for Christ, Incorporated* and *Legacy Freedom, LLC*. Whether through speaking to groups, counseling individuals and families, or writing books, Tammy desires to see people set free with tools of inner healing and relational unity. Tammy and her husband, Bill, live in Fayetteville, GA and have two adult daughters.

To learn more about Tammy Melton or to inquire about booking her for your upcoming speaking engagements, visit legacyministries.info or tammymelton.com

Tammy Melton is available for:

- *Refining Relationships* Retreats
- Inner Healing Prayer Training
- Christian Conferences
- Presentations Tailored to your Needs

Check out Tammy's book, *Loving God with All Five Senses!*

This insightful Bible study is great for either individuals or groups. *Loving God with All Five Senses* shows new Christians as well as seasoned believers how to taste and see that God is good and how we can let Him be our vision and give us discernment. It also warns of the spiritual pitfalls that result when we misuse God's gifts of taste, touch, sight, hearing, and smell.

Order your paperback or kindle edition on

amazon.com or tammymelton.com.

Made in the USA
Columbia, SC
13 May 2021